- You can return this item to any Bournemouth library but not all libraries are open every day.
- Items must be returned on or before the due date. Please note that you will be charged for items returned late.
- Items may be renewed unless requested by another customer.
- Renewals can be made in any library, by telephone, email or online via the website. Your membership card number and PIN will be required.
- Please look after this item - you may be charged for any damage.

Bournemouth
Libraries

www.bournemouth.gc   ·ibraries

D1492358

SUPERMODEL CHEF

Lorraine Pascale

Sue Blackhall

SUPERMODEL CHEF
Lorraine Pascale

metro

Published by Metro Publishing
an imprint of John Blake Publishing Ltd
3 Bramber Court, 2 Bramber Road,
London W14 9PB, England

www.johnblakepublishing.co.uk

www.facebook.com/Johnblakepub **facebook**
twitter.com/johnblakepub **twitter**

First published in hardback in 2013

ISBN: 978-1-78219-472-9

British Library Cataloguing-in-Publication Data:

A catalogue record for this book is available from the British Library.

Design by www.envydesign.co.uk

Printed in Great Britain by CPI Group (UK) Limited

1 3 5 7 9 10 8 6 4 2

Papers used by John Blake Publishing are natural, recyclable products made
from wood grown in sustainable forests. The manufacturing processes conform
to the environmental regulations of the country of origin.

Every attempt has been made to contact the relevant copyright-holders,
but some were unobtainable. We would be grateful if the appropriate people
could contact us.

Contents

Introduction

The words stared back at her; vile and malicious racist taunts that made her stomach turn. What had she done to deserve such a torrent of abuse – words that were now being read by so many? For a moment the woman who had battled against so much over the years decided to shrug off the verbal attacks – the latest in a string of vicious onslaughts in a year. But then, mustering all the reserve she had relied on so many times in the past, she did what she had always done. She fought back. But nothing, it seemed, was to bring an end to it. It was just one challenge in a series of many she had endured from birth.

With a traumatic start to life, an emotionally

battered background of abandonment, continuous conflicts between who she really was and who she wanted to be and betrayal by the man she loved, Lorraine Pascale has battled through it all.

Given up by her birth parents and then adopted, moved from one foster home to another, a survivor of trauma both in her childhood and adult life, divorcee, mother of one and now one of television's most popular chefs, Lorraine has shown that giving up was never an option. When told she couldn't, she did. Which is exactly how she switched from a hugely successful career as a model featuring in some of the most iconic images of the 1990s, to starting right at the bottom as a cook (with several attempts to find her niche in a series of diverse jobs along the way). Today, Lorraine is one of our most successful TV chefs with acclaimed BBC cookery programmes and best-selling books. She has also made the television 'Top Rich' list – one of only two women TV personalities claiming this achievement. But this book also reveals Lorraine's fate and fortunes in other areas of her life. For as well as becoming a wealthy woman through her celebrity success and career as one of the world's top supermodels, she is an astute businesswoman – and owner of companies, some of which are the legacy of her former marriage to a colourful millionaire musician and aristocrat. It's a far cry from the days when she was ironing neighbours' sheets for £1 an hour and wondering where her tumultuous life would lead her. Furthermore, Lorraine, daughter of Caribbean parents, has had to fight against not only critics who have sneered at her 'catwalk to cupcakes' career change, the cynicism of those who still feel 'proper' chefs never come in the shape of a woman, but also sickening racial prejudice. It can be very challenging as the only black, female cook with such a high profile.

But despite her critics, when in the midst of turmoil Lorraine turned her life around, desperately trying to find personal and professional fulfilment – and finding it only through great determination, or in her words 'grit' and 'grafting'. She has experienced bitter times and enjoyed momentous ones. Now, surrounded by those she can finally love and trust, her life is coming together at last. Despite a frenetic lifestyle she still finds time to support charitable causes whenever she can. And as well as protecting those close to her she is a fierce campaigner on behalf of those with whom she can empathise – with particular focus on children in care who hold the dream of finding secure and loving families, and those for whom finding their place in life seems hopeless. Naturally, once a 'latchkey kid' herself, Lorraine puts teaching cooking skills to these children top of her list.

In her 40th year, Lorraine has experienced more than many twice her age. Her story here, with much that has never been revealed before – including the full extent of the racial abuse she suffers, the real reason behind her acrimonious marital break-up, its ensuing complex financial repercussions and the intriguing clash of two Countesses – bears testimony to the fact that despite all the odds being stacked against you there is the chance not only to survive it all but to rise to great things. Once known as the 'smiley model', Lorraine Pascale now has much to genuinely smile about.

CHAPTER 1

Chicken soup, chilli and childhood comfort

Lorraine's interest in cooking began at an early age – and out of the need to fend for herself. Her adoptive parents, Roger and Audrey Woodward, separated when she was three years old meaning she was then brought up by a single mother who worked nights to make ends meet. In fact, so infrequent were the everyday cooked meals that more fortunate children are lucky enough to take for granted, that Lorraine still recalls getting excited at those rare moments of her mother's 'adventurous' cooking such as tandoori chicken, homemade chicken soup (which appears in Lorraine's book *Fast, Fresh and Easy Food* – 'this is not only comforting, filling and healthy, but also tastes fantastic, even though I can never get it as good as my mum does') and hot chilli. But on the whole, for Lorraine's mother, cooking was a luxury for which she had little time and Lorraine and her older brother Jason usually made something to eat from whatever was left in the fridge.

They were typical 'latchkey kids', letting themselves in the house and fending for themselves whenever their mother was out at work. It was, Lorraine said, 'a life of fish fingers, French bread pizza, samosas and corned beef hash – all with chips.' There were no lovingly packed lunches for school either. Every day the young Lorraine staved off hunger with egg mayonnaise sandwiches made with the white bread she detested so much, a packet of crisps and a Kit Kat or Penguin chocolate bar. But even way back then, she had a taste for cakes and pastries, spending her pocket money on chocolate brownies and her favourite Viennese whirls from a bakery on the way to school while the other kids headed for the sweet shop. 'I don't know where my obsession came from,' she has admitted. But even birthdays do not evoke memories of a kitchen full of evocative baking smells. With money short, there was no elaborate shop-bought birthday cake either – just a 'chocolate fridge cake' – a rather bizarre concoction of crushed digestive biscuits mixed in with chocolate and 'set' in the fridge. Poignantly, it is no celebratory meal Lorraine has as a first memory of food, but Shredded Wheat, eaten three at a time and with no milk. In fact, she flatly refused to take milk of any kind when she was a toddler. She still eats her cereals dry.

None of this is to suggest that Lorraine's mother was uncaring, but she had found herself in the quite unexpected situation where she had one natural child and an adopted one to bring up on her own. However, it is perhaps not surprising that schoolgirl Lorraine gravitated towards feeding herself. And that meant early experimentation with whatever makings of a meal were in the house – strangely enough, most usually bread and garlic. So came about one of Lorraine's very first culinary creations. Day after day she would return home and make herself her own special TV-dinner – bread spread with Flora and cubes of garlic – 'loads of garlic' – which she placed under a grill.

But Lorraine would be the last one to say this was a time of hardship. She adored her adoptive mother and despite her parents' divorce she was still close to them both. Although she had shown an interest in the 'magic' of cooking right from the tender age of five – she still fondly remembers taking a battered old tin with a picture of Buckingham Palace on it containing the ingredients to make raspberry buns to her primary school with a teacher who 'was beautiful like Marilyn Monroe' – it was Lorraine's absent father who was to be her inspiration when it came to the simple pleasures of preparing and cooking food. His remarriage to an Italian woman further encouraged him to take to the kitchen and lovingly create what were, for Lorraine, pretty sumptuous meals of roasts and salads – and the Italian staple of pasta dishes.

The taste of one of her father's dishes is still imprinted on Lorraine's memory and literally gave her a taste for spicing up food. She recalled: 'One day when I was about eight, he cooked a pasta dish with huge amounts of chilli and paprika. It was so spicy that it burnt my mouth. I asked him what it was and he said, "It's pasta with an angry sauce."' It was Penne Arrabiata. 'He had sautéed pancetta with garlic and then added tinned tomatoes, paprika and a red chilli with its seeds. I absolutely loved it. It is my dad's favourite dish and one I remember him always cooking. He was always travelling and coming back with ideas for different dishes, especially Spanish and Italian things.' (Including, some might say, an Italian wife!)

During this time Lorraine mainly just watched as her father cooked but she looked and listened, inadvertently storing up knowledge for a culinary life change which as yet was nowhere on her radar. For Lorraine these were special times and just how close they brought her and her father together was highlighted when she eventually found fame as one of television's most popular chefs. The two of them got the chance to cook together in front of the cameras for one of her TV shows and the mutual pride shone through – 'My dad was so up for it! He actually asked me when I was going to be filming so he could do the show, so I did not have to bribe him. I just gave him lots of hugs to make him feel comfy.'

Lorraine's dad helped with the potato wedges and she made 'old-fashioned burgers'. Though as someone who is meant to be such a good cook, Roger undoubtedly threw Lorraine when she asked him on screen how he made his own burgers and he replied: 'I usually buy them!' It was just a short time on TV together, a tasting of their wares straight from the barbecue, but it confirmed Lorraine's closeness to the man she calls 'Popsicle', which has continued into adult life. 'Dad's Penne Arrabiata' was also to feature in Lorraine's *Fast, Fresh and Easy Food* cookbook and was no doubt tried and tested by her followers. And only one Italian fan pointed out that the correct name should be '*Penne all'Arrabbiata*'...

And so the majority of Lorraine's treats of home-cooked, tasty meals were savoured not actually at home but on visits to her father, whom she visited at weekends and during the school holidays. Holidays with him in the summer were a special highlight for the little girl. They would go on camping trips to Normandy and Brittany, where purchases of baguettes, peppercorn pâté, ham, salad, cheese and tomatoes made the perfect childhood memory of picnics in a beautiful setting with the sun warming their backs. It was during one of these idyllic holidays that Lorraine had her first encounter with one of the simple, but tricky, delights of French restaurant dining. Thinking it simply sounded a nice thing to try, Lorraine ordered a seafood platter – a mountain of clams and mussels with no obvious way of actually cracking into it! A kindly French waiter showed her the way the locals did it – using a mussel shell to extract the edible bits. A tricky challenge, but it initiated Lorraine into yet another culinary experience at an early age.

Lorraine has enjoyed many a fine meal since then (the best, she claimed, was at London's Le Gavroche – pan-fried foie gras and 'the best beef I have ever eaten'), but it is those simple, unsophisticated mealtime memories from childhood that she savours most.

Later life brought the chance to travel further afield and Lorraine used her eating experiences as a basis for what would eventually lead her into a highly successful cooking career. She still picks up any knowledge of local dishes when she goes abroad and admits that she is forever on the look-out for new ideas, especially ones involving spices and fresh and unusual ingredients. And several of her TV programmes see her visiting other countries like France and Spain for inspiration, much of which forms the basis for the recipes she includes in her series and bestselling books.

Lorraine has said that before she travels abroad, she researches the best restaurants on her itinerary and, being the well-organised person she is, will book a table in advance. She doesn't just go for the more expensive ones, but also chooses, 'really good value ones'. As well as her early visit to Barcelona where she sampled tapas for the very first time – 'dishes like patatas bravas, prawns in oil, a plate of chorizo and heaps of garlic and paprika which were just so me' – Lorraine was later to find herself in the fortunate position of travelling to locations such as Cambodia, Laos, Thailand and Vietnam. For by this time the financial rewards from her modelling, combined with her divorce settlement, gave her the chance to pick her destinations (rather than have them dictated by modelling assignments) as she had never done before.

Australia, the place she was visiting when she made the decision to drop out of school and drop into modelling, is still a regular destination, though her busy life meant she made her first visit there in five years at the end of 2011, a trip that also took in Los Angeles and Sri Lanka. A year later, in December 2012, Lorraine was back to film *MasterChef Australia* – one of her own personal favourite cookery programmes (over there she has been described as a 'spunky English chef') – as one of the guest chefs and made her Mojito Genoese cake. As ever, Lorraine had her fans: 'This week, as soon as Gary [one of the judges, Gary Megihan] introduced the guest "chef" as an ex-model, I knew Ms Pascale would sashay through the kitchen with a big smile towards her KitchenAid.' And one of the contestants said he found it hard to listen to Lorraine's constructive advice on how to ice cakes because she was leaning over in a top (pink instead of her usual pristine white) that revealed a nice view of her cleavage!

Both trips eased the Australia 'withdrawal symptoms' Lorraine said she was getting, as she now sees the country as more than the location for the *Home and Away* and *Neighbours* soaps she watched as a teenager and is completely smitten. She still recalls the thrill of her first sighting of the Sydney Opera House – 'It literally took my breath away. And it still does; that Opera House gets me every time.' She has made good friends through her visits to Melbourne (the first Australian city she visited) and Sydney. Her closest friends are centred around Byron Bay in New South Wales and when Lorraine visits she often stays at a boutique hotel owned by one of her friends: 'I've met some cool people and travelled around. Some of my friends call me their honorary Aussie.'

In fact, for Lorraine, the perfect Christmas would be spent on the beach at Byron Bay 'staring at the ocean, cooking a barramundi [a type of fish] on the barbecue served simply with lemon, lime and butter. Christmas lunch as good as it gets.' Australian cookery fans marvel at how Lorraine has 'built, iced and decorated a reputation as one of the best bakers in the biz.' She in turn has brought some of the country's recipes to the tables of Great Britain, including Australian bread – 'traditionally, I am led to believe, made by people in the bush on the campfire.'

Lorraine took her daughter Ella, then aged nine, on the six-week 'gastronomic tour' of Asia. The two of them went on cookery courses, gleaning skills and new tastes from classes held in hotels and 'home-stays' where local families passed on their recipes. It all added up to a very special experience. 'One night we had red beef Thai curry and the cook said we probably wouldn't want it spicy because we were European, but I said we liked things spicy. It blew my head off!' A slightly less hot version of this particular dish was later to find its way into one of Lorraine's cookbooks. One dish that did not make it was the deep-fried insects they had eaten at a roadside stall in Thailand – 'It was a bit grim but we were ravenous and there was so much batter on them you couldn't really taste anything…' But while that experience might have put Lorraine off, the generally well-spiced and exotic approach to cooking certainly did not. It enthralled her, and Thailand (as well as Australia) has 'hosted' Lorraine for Christmas over the years.

So cooking back then was beginning to take its hold on Lorraine. But in future years it was to become in many ways her escape and therapy: 'You feel most authentically yourself. All my memories of childhood are definitely through food...'

Chapter 2

Finding a family

Lorraine was 18 months old when her Caribbean birth parents – of Jamaican and St Lucian origins – gave her up for adoption following problems in their relationship. Being so tiny, she has few memories of what life with her real mother and father was like, but today still carries the sad memories of the unsettled life that followed. Literally having just found her feet as a toddler, she was uprooted from her London home. Unusually, Lorraine was not taken into care for any period of time before being adopted. She went straight to a white middle-class couple, Roger and Audrey Woodward in Witney, Oxfordshire. The pair had married in Amersham in 1961 and had a son,

Jason, who was three years older than Lorraine. She feels that perhaps her adoptive parents were chosen because they had once lived and worked in Jamaica. (Interestingly, a Roger Woodward teaching at St Jago High School, Spanish Town, St Catherine, was called as a witness to a murder there in 1964.)

Lorraine's academic adoptive father had also been a Spanish teacher at Oxford College (Lorraine is proud to note that he speaks seven languages) and her adoptive mother was a nurse. She was also, Lorraine has said, 'very inspirational'. In fact, her mother, in a move that probably taught Lorraine to persevere with her dreams, claimed free flying lessons in payment for working at a flying school and went on to become one of the first female pilots in Britain. Most importantly, Lorraine was being given the chance to retrieve the family life she had lost. Because of their time in Jamaica, the Woodwards were always aware of the Caribbean culture, taking Lorraine to related events and to the local Baptist church so that she could meet other Caribbean people. 'They didn't want to ignore my colour, but at the same time, they didn't want to make a big deal out of it. So it never seemed a big deal to me.'

The visits proved useful in other ways. 'My mum would ask the women for advice on my hair because dealing with an Afro is a challenge when you have no experience of it.' In the end, Lorraine's mother found a rather drastic answer to tearing at the Afro fuzz with a comb every day before school. She gave Lorraine a bit of a shearing! 'She decided she couldn't deal with it and shaved it all off. She didn't give me a number one – I still had a bit of coverage. I was just glad that I didn't have to get my hair ripped out every day and grateful that I didn't have FA Cup ears!'

Then, in a trauma no methodical assessment by social workers could have predicted, Roger and Audrey Woodward split up when Lorraine was just three years old. The man who had become 'dad' in Lorraine's eyes moved out. Lorraine remained with her mother, who endeavoured to make sure the little girl would have as normal a life as possible (there is lovely picture of Lorraine dressed in her uniform as a member of the Girls Brigade when she was five). When she was older, Lorraine and her big brother Jason would often go on bike rides together to open fields just a few minutes away. Sometimes they would be out all day. It was a time when children had the freedom to go out on such expeditions with no threat. Lorraine remembers: 'We used to head out in the morning and not come home until the evening. I have no idea what we ate!' Those safe, summer days seem idyllic.

But adjusting to a ready-made – and white – brother took some doing. 'It felt different having a brother who was my parents' blood child. I couldn't say how exactly, but it did feel different. I just remember Jason and I having a normal relationship and arguing like brothers and sisters do. He was older so I'd follow him around and copy him, and he didn't like it – you know, the usual. I don't think we spoke about my adoption.' But Lorraine, who had already experienced the loss of her two biological parents and the separation of her adoptive ones, was to endure more drastic change in her young life. When she was eight she had her first experience of the care system when her mother became ill – an illness Lorraine has said her mother does not want discussed.

Lorraine was placed with a foster family. With what appears to be some lack of thought by the authorities – although the family was already known to Lorraine and also had an adopted daughter she knew – the kindly couple, who had some experience with both fostering and adoption, were also just round the corner from her old home. Lorraine considered this to be 'lucky', as she could at least remain in her hometown. It also meant she kept running back 'home' to have tea with her brother and to try to re-establish contact with her mother. But it was not considered to be the right situation for Lorraine and so she was moved again. She has described this decision as 'one of the many mysteries of fostering' because she had liked the close proximity of the place and the people she knew as home. What Lorraine must have seen as yet another temporary set of parents came into her life, this time 15 miles away. Another family. Another set of rules. Another mother and father who expected Lorraine to adapt to it all. Former missionaries, the couple insisted she go to church with them every day – 'not necessarily top of your list when you're eight...' In a deeply personal interview with *The Times*, Lorraine described what she felt was a politically correct, though not necessarily suitable, placement: 'They were white. And they were very religious. And this is just my take on it, but in their house, as you walked in, there were zebra rugs on the floor and African carved scary things, and I think the social worker went "Ooh, fabulous, black child, zebra rug, animal heads, fantastic. Perfect match. They've been in Africa, great." And so I went there. And they were wonderful people, but the match wasn't right.'

Lorraine was not comfortable with her weekly meetings with a social worker during these troubled times. She had nothing to say. She didn't want to talk; she didn't have an answer when asked how she was. 'I just wanted to get to the part where she'd buy me a bun and I'd lick the icing off...'

Lorraine was eventually reunited with her adoptive mother. By this time her father had re-married – to Katie – and Lorraine had a half-sister, Francesca. She had kept up the close relationship with her father (she has said that her 'best ever' Christmas present was from him – a 'Girls World' doll's head on which you could create different hairstyles, when she was six – 'even though I soon ruined it by cutting the hair off'). But the feelings of abandonment and rejection still haunt her. First she was given up by her birth parents, and then those who had taken her on as their own child were unable to maintain the normal parenting security. Then there was the being moved around with no real sense of belonging and the insecurity of just who would be the people she could permanently call 'mum' and 'dad'. Although that craved-for security and stable family finally materialised in adult life, it is no wonder that Lorraine is forever wary. And her recollection of those unsettled days is heartbreaking. 'Abandonment is the big issue. If you've had a ruptured childhood things can be hard in adult life. You find it hard to make attachments,' she has said. 'It was a pretty grim childhood. In your mind, your bags are always packed as you never know how long you're going to be anywhere. It's hard to forge close bonds with people as you're never told whether you'll be with a family for weeks, months or years.'

Lorraine was obviously aware that she was being brought up by people who were not her birth parents. She said: 'I knew I was adopted from the start. My parents were white and I was black but you don't think of that when you are a child. My mother just told me all the time that I was adopted but I didn't actually know what it meant. People say it must have been odd, but I didn't know any different. I accepted it because it was all so open, which I think is the best way to be.' Describing herself as a 'child of the 1970s', Lorraine feels that her later years growing up in London and then taking off to different parts of the world helped her put the whole colour thing into perspective. People are just people, no matter what their origins are. 'I see beyond colour or even thinking like that,' she has said.

Every adopted child is curious about its origins and Lorraine was no different. She needed to know exactly why her parents had forsaken her. Their decision would see her endure feelings of abandonment and would set her on a path of ensuing childhood upheaval. All the explanation her adoptive mother could offer when Lorraine asked why she was given up was that it was for 'personal reasons'. In fact, Lorraine was one of four children but the other three are really 'half siblings' for she was conceived during a relationship her mother had during a separation from her father and was later given up for adoption when the two got back together again. Nothing about Lorraine's early years was straightforward – or pain-free. And there was more to come.

It is not surprising that her experiences as a child have shaped the way Lorraine is today. She has had to toughen up even though her self-esteem was knocked so many times. 'My childhood experiences didn't make me more confident; less confident actually. But they also made me more resilient, more independent, more of a grafter. They also made me able to look after myself, to be self-sufficient and not have to depend on others.'

It was with this backdrop of upheaval and uncertainty that Lorraine must have considered why she was then on the move again. When she was 11, the age when children move on from primary to secondary school, Lorraine did not make what would have appeared to be the most natural transition to a secondary school in her local 'catchment area'. Instead, she was granted a full scholarship to a boarding school in Devon. The school was one of two that takes children on scholarships in that county under a nationwide scheme specialising in giving opportunities to children who have been in care or who are from dysfunctional families.

Lorraine's particular opportunity came via the Frank Buttle Trust, which gives grant aid to children and young people whom it describes as being in 'desperate need' or those with 'medical, emotional or social difficulties to gain a stable and more supportive secondary education'. It is the largest UK charity to do this and those eligible for its help include adopted children, children cared for by grandparents or other relatives and friends, and orphaned children. (It also, incidentally, provides support through the BBC Children in Need Small Grants Scheme.) The national scheme, where possible and when it is deemed suitable, endeavours to place a child in a school within their local authority. There were obviously reasons why Lorraine was awarded a place out of her home area, but some years later she was to recognise the Trust's support, saying: 'Buttle UK helped me in the past. Their support gave me the opportunity to develop and thrive after a difficult start in life. I owe such a lot today to that experience, and I am supporting Buttle UK so many more children can benefit like I did.' Her gratitude came in 2013 when she helped with the Buttle's Great Bake Challenge to mark the Trust's 60th anniversary and described it as 'a wonderful cause'.

Though uneasy about yet again leaving the familiarity of what was now a fairly settled life with her mother and brother, Lorraine knew she had been given a chance to thrive and it was one that would bring her a close circle of good friends. She was, in the main, a good pupil with only the occasional streak of rebellion. 'I was quite square at school. At one point I started being naughty and they contacted my mother and said that if I continued to misbehave they would take the scholarship off me and the money would have to be paid back. So I stopped being naughty. I didn't want to be faced with the wrath of my mother...' One school report from 1985 describes Lorraine as being 'very enthusiastic' but also very messy, adding, 'Her desk always seems too small.' It continued, 'We hope that next term she will learn to concentrate, be more patient and work on improving her scarcely legible handwriting.'

That Lorraine's teachers had only these minor criticisms to make was in itself very telling of her determination to fit in at the school and make use of her time there. For there are occasions in this innovative scheme, which depends so heavily on both a school's readiness to participate and the ability of a troubled child to adapt, when it simply doesn't work out. But Lorraine, despite no doubt having initial reservations, made it work. A fairly good all-rounder, even at this tender age she shone in her home economics lessons. She would have taken the subject at A-level had she not been 'discovered' by a model agency scout. For a 16-year-old the modelling world was an offer too good to refuse, and as Lorraine has admitted, it got her out of sleepy Witney (she went home most weekends), back into London – and then New York. She had the support of her parents who did not demur when Lorraine said she would not be returning to school. But there are times when she regrets her choice and wonders what might have happened had she continued her studies; a choice which almost inevitably would have seen her go on to further education with its accompanying opportunity to grow in confidence. 'I always felt that by not going to university I'd missed out. Not just on education but also on a chance to find out more about myself and figure out what really makes me tick.'

Lorraine was fortunate to find herself in an adoptive family – albeit one that was soon to be divided – which would provide her with a loving and supportive grounding for the rest of her life. Today, she is still very close to her adoptive mother and father in their separate lives. Her father is a strong figure, always there for her in the background, and her mother, too, remains a caring influence. 'My mother has always been very honest and open, which I think is so important with children. She has been supportive of whatever I've wanted to do in life.'

But Lorraine is perhaps understandably cynical about the whole adoptive system and speaks straight from her heart. 'The focus is wrong. It's on a nice, well-off family, but if the parents don't have the skills to deal with the emotion this can lead to terrible things. It doesn't matter how great, how old, or what colour they are... one day I hope that the powers that be will realise that love above all else is what matters to children needing homes. Love and stability...' In other words, children should feel they belong, and not, as Lorraine has said, have to keep 'packing your bag' and being on the move from one family to another.

Lorraine has admitted to researching her background. It was to present her with an agonising dilemma. Should she try to make contact with her biological parents and siblings? Or should she leave the past alone? In the end, she decided that there would be no purpose in seeing the parents who gave her up when she was still virtually just a baby. She said: 'I know where they are, who they are. I could find them tomorrow if I wanted, but I don't. I don't feel that after a meeting with them my life will suddenly make sense.' And there will always be gaps, with Lorraine never having had the chance to find out even the most basic elements of her natural roots and birth family – details enjoyed by those whose lives have not been splintered in the way hers has.

Said Lorraine: 'People who know their biological parents know their medical history. They have a rough idea of what's happened in the family – when people died, and how. It's a mirror of what might happen to them. It's occurred to me that I don't know anything. What if everyone in my family dies at 40? I just don't know.' She would never know, either, where her life would have led, had she enjoyed a normal, happy and loving existence with her real parents. And here, her background could be seen as a double-edged sword. If she had grown up with her birth parents she would, of course, never have experienced the trauma that accompanied her childhood, but perhaps there would not have been the inclination to really push herself to make her mark. Would she have become the strong and successful woman she now is had she not had to contend with the ensuing experiences and repercussions of that unsettled period in her life? There may not have been the decision to go into the precarious but dazzling world of modelling. There would not have been the marriage, which although failing, did give her added financial independence – and the daughter she adores. There might not even have been the same grit and determination that has carried her through to the success she now enjoys. Perhaps often feeling like a nobody has made Lorraine Pascale into a somebody.

It is no wonder that her experiences were to leave Lorraine emotionally scarred. She knew she had been given away by her natural parents, she had suffered the turmoil of a second splintered family, temporarily lost the woman who had become her loving replacement mother, and she had been re-homed with those who could only provide short-term security. Said Lorraine: 'I'm not sure if I knew at eight that being with foster parents was a temporary thing. I'm sure I did, but there are always the issues of abandonment when it comes to adoption and fostering.'

She uses the emotive word 'abandonment' often,

and with good reason. Anyone who has been through the adoption process desperate to know about their real parents and with the added agony of wondering why they were just not good enough to keep, will empathise with Lorraine's feeling of having no real identity and with having none of the childhood memories most are lucky enough to have with their birth mother and father. It is painful beyond belief. 'I'd watch TV and think, "Oh, that nurse on *Casualty* looks a bit like me," and I'd wait for the credits to see her name,' Lorraine has said. 'Realising I'm black and my family is white was a gradual thing for me. I remember seeing Michael Jackson in the *Thriller* video and thinking, "Look, we're the same colour." Seeing him made me wonder what was going on and when I asked my mum she told me, "You didn't come from my tummy, you came from another mummy's tummy..."'

With such painful memories of adoption, it's not surprising that Lorraine fully understands other children who have shared the same experience. She is a stalwart campaigner to make the whole process more compassionate, more aware of each individual child's plight and needs, but above all to spare those concerned the trauma and feeling of 'not belonging' which she herself has suffered. There is, of course, the added prejudice of a face that doesn't fit because it's a different colour...

One of Lorraine's foster families got in touch with her via Facebook and Lorraine responded. 'I haven't seen them since I was nine although we did become close, but they wanted to say "hello". They're really proud of me, which is lovely.' Although nowadays it is easier for adopted children to make contact with their birth parents, this is not something Lorraine has the desire to do. Despite the tentative contact she did not feel there was any point in trying to re-establish a relationship. It has been that way since the day they decided they could not keep her. 'Now there are open adoptions and the children stay in contact with the family, but it wasn't like that for me. I know my birth parents' names, I know I've got three brothers and one sister, I know that some of them are in London but I don't have any desire or need to find them. One family is enough.'

Lorraine has said that she feels she is one of the 'rare few' who don't feel the need to find the missing pieces of her background 'puzzle'. She doesn't even know if her 'birth family' fully realise that the eighteen-month-old they gave up for adoption is the beautiful, successful and famous woman on television.

Chapter 3

From the classroom to the catwalk

Lorraine was just 15 when fate would dramatically change her life from being a normal schoolgirl to something far more glamorous. Myth has it that she was on a day off from boarding school and with a friend visiting the filming of television's *The Clothes Show* in Plymouth, Devon, when, on the spur of the moment she decided to enter a modelling contest. The story goes that despite having looks to equal those of black supermodel Naomi Campbell (Lorraine was already tall), complete with striking figure, face – and yes, even similar teeth – Lorraine was told that her look was just not right for the moment.

In fact, Lorraine was in London's Covent Garden

'trailing behind my friends' when a representative from a model agency who saw the potential in the lanky schoolgirl with the engaging smile thrust a card into her hands telling her she should try modelling. Lorraine recalled: 'She said she was a professional model scout and I thought, "Oh yeah, this is a bit dubious," but she told me they were a member of the Association of Model Agencies and were bona fide and asked me to check them out, which I did. I called them, and that was it.' Well, it wasn't quite it, for the agency whose scout had approached Lorraine actually then told her they couldn't represent her.

At the time she contacted that first agency, Lorraine had given no thought to modelling as a career and certainly had no intention of giving up school early to do so. But that initial approach had put the idea into her head. She contacted several other agencies, inadvertently including one specialising in topless models – 'I saw a picture of Samantha Fox on the wall and quietly slipped out.' But her perseverance paid off and she was finally signed up by one, Profile, which also had the up-and-coming young model Naomi Campbell on their books. Here, Lorraine was to make a big impression from the very first sighting.

Susanne Fredricks, then head booker of the 'New Faces' department of Profile, recalled the first time she saw Lorraine: 'As she walked through the door, I knew we were going to take her on. She was, tall, slender, and absolutely stunning. Her bone structure was exquisite, as was her complexion, and she possessed this effortless grace at such a young age.' But as well as the compliments the teenage Lorraine was briefed on the pitfalls and demands. 'She was, of course, interested in modelling, as all young girls are, but it's not an easy road to take. It requires not only the "look" but resilience, commitment and the hard work that go-sees and castings demand. A model must also be comfortable in front of a camera, and be able to bring life and energy to her work,' said Fredricks.

Having taken the teenager on their books, Profile then set about creating her new image. Fredricks took Lorraine shopping for a basic wardrobe to wear on the endless round of appointments – all arranged to accommodate her school schedule. Said Fredricks: 'Once we had discussed how we could work with Lorraine around her education priorities we moved into styling her before we sent her out on any appointments. We shopped for the Levi jeans and white T-shirts we initiated new girls into as a set simplicity of style – unless a casting or appointment was more specific.' It was also Fredricks who sat down and talked to Lorraine's parents about how their daughter could take her first tentative steps into a modelling career while not abandoning school altogether. 'The main priority in the beginning was maintaining her education whilst she began her career.

We had always agreed that her education was of prime importance. After meeting with her adopted parents we decided a way forward that they were happy with.' For Lorraine it was also the opportunity to 'get out of my little town – although I do love Witney – and go to London and see the bright lights'.

After being formally signed up to the agency, there then followed more rounds of photographers, advertisers and magazines. And it was certainly no overnight fame for Lorraine. 'A lot of models join an agency and their careers take off, they just fly. But for me it was a lot of hard graft, a lot of knocking on doors and rejection. It is incredibly difficult. Sometimes I was given a list of ten appointments I had to make for the day. There would be times when they would look through all my portfolio and times when they would only look at three of the ten pages and just say "thank you very much".' The fashion industry, she discovered, was only interested in a certain look. And, at a time when white girls were monopolising the scene – Naomi Campbell being the exception, of course – many believed Lorraine just did not have it.

No model is without their very personal CV and Lorraine had one too. Hers for Profile, the agency who originally signed her up, read as follows:

Nationality: British (English)
Hair colour: Black

Eye colour: Brown
Date of birth: May 11th 1973
Height: 5' 10.5"; 179cm
Measurements: (US) 34-24-34; (EU) 86.5-61-86.5
Dress size: (US) 4; (EU) 41; (UK) 7

Lorraine's place of birth was left empty. For some reason her date of birth is wrong. It is actually 17 November 1972, the date given on later agency details. Obviously this new life needed a new name. 'Woodward', the surname taken from her adoptive parents, was deemed not exotic enough. And so Lorraine Pascale was chosen. This was a relatively easy decision as Pascale is Lorraine's middle name – and it had just the right ring about it for a model. Or as Susanne Fredricks put it: 'It had more of a "vine" to it so that's what we decided to roll with.' The name, incidentally, is Italian of origin (and comes from an old, distinguished family) and was originally the name for anyone born on Easter Day.

Fredricks has said it was she who persuaded Lorraine to have her wild Afro hair cut into the complete crop that was to provide many dramatic images during Lorraine's modelling career. She took the teenage aspiring model to stylist Eugene Souleiman at the Trevor Sorbie salon. Out would go Lorraine's natural, wayward hair and in came a head that was virtually shaved. 'She was reluctant at first, but was quite thrilled with the final result! It was a tight crop, and showed the beauty of her face. The hairstyle was decided upon as she was first launched into the market.'

Lorraine's dramatic new look obviously presented a striking image and she was booked for her first editorial within a week. Her 'scalping' was a particularly brave decision, particularly when she hit New York. For around this time when black models were still fighting to make their mark, they were complaining that they had to wear their hair long and straight 'like white models'. But her early success was also certainly recognition of Lorraine's natural beauty, for part of the Profile 'overhaul' was to send her out on appointments bare-faced, completely free of make-up, to show off her inherent glow and clear skin. It was also recognition of the confidence the young model was projecting. Fredricks has said even at this early age, Lorraine was 'always a very assured young woman. Intelligent, focused and authentic.'

Lorraine, now aged 16, managed for a while to juggle her education with the start of her modelling career. Model shoots were scheduled around her schooling where possible – she was in the middle of her GCSEs – but she was still missing out on some modelling jobs. So something had to give. But Lorraine admitted that she didn't feel the great pull to carry on at school. (Though she is still conscious of gaps in her education, particularly English grammar, and says she is not 'much of a wordsmith'.) Despite enjoying the nurturing environment of the Devon boarding school, she has said she wasn't really academic – one of her GCSE successes was a grade B for Textiles – but she was later to express regret at not having carried on with her education, saying that 16 was not old enough to cope with the pressures of modelling. 'It was too young, not just because you don't just need school but you need the whole socialising thing and learning how to become an adult.'

Some years later, in 2009, Lorraine reiterated her feelings about the difficulties surrounding young models. She was attending the launch of a re-release of a book by Julian Short called *A Model for Living: The Aspiring Supermodel's Self Help Guide* (published originally in Australia four years earlier under the title *An Intelligent Life*). The book was a 'useful guide for advising new models and their families about various aspects of the industry'. Described as the 'Nineties über-model', Lorraine commented: 'This is a great book – it offers positive advice about dealing with difficult and everyday situations. As a model, this would have been an invaluable guide for me when I was starting out and meeting different people, travelling, and being away from home and family. It also offers practical advice for maintaining a healthy self-esteem and learning to be confident, and this is really important for today's young models – and women in general.'

Lorraine was actually on an extended summer holiday in Australia with friends when she finally made the decision not to return to school; a decision her parents eventually backed, despite the fact she was scheduled to take her A-level exams. It was time for another sit-down talk with Lorraine's parents. Said Fredricks: 'I really didn't persuade them except to say Lorraine's potential for success in the industry was very promising. They had already seen this during Lorraine's time with us.'

But Lorraine's parents, especially her father Roger, were at first not convinced. Being an academic, he was, she has said, 'not too pleased' at her decision but she had already started to earn 'really good money' and believed that perhaps she could go back to school later.

Lorraine had been with Profile for just over a year when, in tribute to her professionalism and growing appeal, she was offered a contract with 'rival' model agency Models One. There was another difficult decision to be made, for Lorraine had been happy with Profile and was torn between leaving the agency that had launched her career and nurtured her from the start, and going to one which promised her big things. Said Fredricks: 'Although my boss was obviously trying to get her to stay with us and

Lorraine was reluctant to go, she and I decided it was in her best interests long term.'

There was another reason why Lorraine found the idea of leaving Profile particularly hard. She and Fredricks, herself then only 19, had forged a firm friendship. Fredricks is Jamaican and the two had developed a strong bond 'due to my knowledge of her heritage from which she felt disconnected'. Fredricks added: 'I wasn't much older than her so I was very much sisterly energy for her. She wanted to stay at Profile mostly due to our relationship, I think, but I encouraged her to take the opportunity as it would be more fast track and secure for her.' And so Lorraine left. But she and Fredricks stayed in touch for several years, losing contact only when Lorraine's modelling career, already seeing her take to the catwalk in Europe, took her to New York.

Fredricks, now a curator at an art gallery in Jamaica, still has fond memories of the nervous schoolgirl who had the courage to walk through Profile's doors. 'She was a very bright and engaging youngster and I always felt she would be successful in whatever she chose to do.' She also recalled how much Lorraine's parents had backed their daughter: 'She had the support of her parents emotionally and I think this is what gave her the confidence and stability to be able to take the risks she did.'

There were certainly risks, for Lorraine was still

trying to make it in an industry where models with her coloured skin were not hot favourites. However, she was soon to become one. 'Back in the late 1980s there weren't many black models in the industry, and she proceeded to become one of the most in-demand,' said Fredricks. In later life Lorraine would talk about the importance of taking risks, saying that for her, it was all about having the inner strength to embrace change. On this occasion that resolve certainly worked and Lorraine was to be booked for various shows at the prestigious London, Paris and Milan Fashion Weeks. Monitoring her prodigy's blossoming career, Fredricks was delighted when, just after a year, Lorraine's career 'catapulted even further' and she found still more success in New York.

One of Lorraine's first American catwalk shows was on 1 April 1990 when she modelled for no payment for an AIDS benefit show at New York's Tribeca Grill. She had accepted the request from designer Kim West, whose clothes have featured in many magazines, including *Vogue,* and been worn by, amongst others, Madonna and Kylie Minogue. Kim West Clothing (which was later to be known for its 'signature' use of Latex) had only been established for six years when West approached Lorraine to take part in the charity show organised by Deborah Shaw of personal stylist company Shaws Solutions. West was delighted that 'Lorraine graciously volunteered' to model for her – and was no doubt impressed about just how good she looked as she strutted the catwalk in a skin-hugging white catsuit. But this was certainly no low-key affair. The AIDS Benefit Fashion Show was one of a series of events described as a 'big budget extravaganza' (Madonna performed at a benefit concert) and was aimed at not only raising money to beat AIDS but also highlighted the deaths of several designers from the disease.

Back in the late 1980s, AIDS was still pretty much something of a taboo but it touched the fashion world, as well as the entertainment business. As Joyce Saenz Harris commented in the *Dallas Morning News*: 'The fashion industry often has been accused of shallowness, of focusing on surfaces and appearances rather than on realities. But in the 1980s, fashion has come face-to-face with a reality so harsh that it threatens the very future of the business.'

Today Kim West is still one of Lorraine's 'followers' and is pleased the teenage model who gave her time so generously, is doing 'fantastically well' and looking 'as fabulous as ever'.

Lorraine later signed up with another agency, Storm, where her modelling details – height, colour of hair and statistics – although matching those of Profile, omitted her birth date. Here, there might be some licence over exactly how old she was when she entered the modelling world. For Lorraine says she was 18 when she met Storm's owner, Sarah Doukas, in 1992 (if her birth year of 1972 is correct, she would of course have been 20). Another interview with Rose Millard for the *Radio Times* in 2011 waxing lyrical about Lorraine being 'fabulously photogenic, with a rather glam hinterland' said she was aged 38. (In fact, Lorraine celebrated her 40th birthday in 2012.)

Storm's professional but non-business-like approach appealed to Lorraine. It was, she said, the family feel with Sarah 'at the helm as mother' that clinched it for her to go on their books. Promotional material for Storm says it plans 'each person's career for the long term, always taking individual strengths and personal circumstances into account. This, we believe, will maximise potential, job satisfaction and help create opportunities. We also build strong client relationships endeavouring always to represent the most exciting modelling talent.'

In an interview about mentors in *Red Magazine*, Lorraine spoke of her trust in and closeness to Doukas. 'She completely believed that I'd be a big success, but more than that she seemed to care about me personally. Sarah's very maternal – she always wanted to know how my personal life was, or what my dreams and aspirations were.' Although Lorraine was now that bit older, Doukas still kept a maternal eye on her and has expressed her amazement at how she and other school leavers handled going into such a demanding business at a tender age. Said Doukas: 'To go off to do the shows at 16 – New York, Milan, Paris – the craziness of it all is so much I don't know how someone aged 21 does it, let alone aged 16.'

Lorraine has said that during her time at Storm the two women spoke two or three times a day. 'There might be a big work project to discuss, but she always makes time to chat about my home life too. She's always one of the first to know of any boyfriends or if I'm feeling poorly.' The friendship was further forged when Doukas, instead of dissuading Lorraine to stay, encouraged her to follow her dream of being a chef. 'Many agents might have been short-sighted, wanting me to keep earning money, but Sarah was excited by my branching out and taking a risk. She wanted me to think bigger.'

A major part of Lorraine's modelling career was spent in New York. She was there for seven years and worked with many of the world's top designers. Her first visit there, however, was not without a few problems. Just 18 and not at all worldly wise when she landed at JFK International Airport, she was casually dressed and seems to have given rise to suspicions from the authorities that there might be something of an undesirable alien in their midst. Although not being perfectly turned out does not seem to warrant the treatment that Lorraine was then to suffer – including the threat of what immigration staff classify as an 'intimate search'. Said Lorraine: 'I didn't know that you shouldn't dress like a scruff bag when you arrive in the United States. The immigration person said, "Will you come this way, please," and took me into this side room. Then she said, "Could you remove all of your clothes, please" and she started to put her rubber gloves on. Then this guardian angel colleague of hers arrived and said, "That's not necessary", and swiftly led me out. I didn't get as far as taking my clothes off, but there was a moment when I wanted to start crying.' It was not an auspicious welcome to America.

But for the following years, Lorraine lived the high life in New York, a city she describes as 'lively and buzzing'. She mixed with the likes of big name actors Robert De Niro and Mickey Rourke in Manhattan's club scene. She shared centre stage with Kate Moss (another Sarah Doukas discovery), Naomi Campbell, Christy Turlington and Cindy Crawford. (There is also a bizarre website claim that says Lorraine founded the New York-based Endometriosis Foundation of America!) But this was also a time of mixed blessings for Lorraine. No matter how glamorous is the place you call home, a model's life can also be a lonely one, with the almost inevitable feelings of isolation in between socialising and waiting for the call to your next job.

'It was exciting but there were also lots of times

when I wasn't doing anything, just sitting around waiting for the phone to ring. I'd jet off on a fabulous trip somewhere exotic, then come back and sit in front of the TV in the flat I was sharing with other models. It's a stop-start life and if you enjoy being busy, which I do, it can be frustrating,' Lorraine has said. But she has admitted that despite the downfalls it did feel 'incredibly special' at the time. 'I would be at these big shows like Chanel, walking out with all the supers, and I knew I was very lucky.' But unlike a lot of the supermodel breed, while others were out partying Lorraine preferred to be at home a lot of the time.

There is a surprising lack of press coverage for Lorraine during this time, with the likes of Naomi and Kate getting in the news but not her. Though one insider said: 'You have to be a really big British name to be in the news in America. Otherwise they don't seem to take much notice.' Lorraine obviously did go to some of the big parties and events, but when she did socialise, she was the sensible one – 'I was never the party animal, maybe because of what my childhood was like. But I always had to be in control. I was the one getting everyone home safely.'

Lorraine has said that the model world was also 'quite transitional' with each new job usually meaning a new group of people to work with. And because of this it was difficult to form really good friendships. But what did stand her in good stead was her childhood experiences with her rather sad description of growing up – going from 'home to home' – which had made her independent. 'I was used to being on my own so it didn't seem a big deal for me. I absolutely loved it.'

Lorraine graced several magazine covers during her modelling time: Spanish *Elle* (March 1991) in a rather awkward-looking arched back pose behind Spanish model Tereza Maxová. Another appearance in *Elle*, the US edition, was in 1993 with the 'It's a Charmed Life' fashion spread which had a discreetly naked top half of Lorraine adorned with Indian-style chains and bangles. She appeared in Britain's *i-D* magazine (July 1991) with a very toothy grin captured by Hugh Stewart and again in April 1996 with a cheeky wink snapped by Craig McDean and in the time of influential fashion editor Edward Enninful. In March 1994 Lorraine graced the front covers of both the Canadian and American editions of *Elle*. The latter was something of a landmark appearance as she was the first black woman ever to appear on its cover. One of a trio, she posed alongside models Avalon Hodges and Jaime Rishar. That cover, together with other vintage *Elle* magazines containing pictures of Lorraine, is now up for sale through eBay.

Getting on the cover of magazines at this time was still quite an achievement for a black model, with agency boss and former model Bethann Hardison commenting that magazines reported they did not sell as well with a black model on the front. Linda Wells of *Allure* magazine agreed: 'Covers are a real problem. Sales are significantly lower when we put a person of color on the cover. I don't know how to change the magazine-buying habits of the consumer. We're in a situation right now where only four or five models sell. I could try to put out a greater number of covers with people of color, but sales are my report card, and I could lose my job if they fail to meet expectations.'

Indeed, coloured girls in the whole modelling scene were treated in a pretty fickle way. Veronica Webb, supermodel at the time, commented: 'When 1996 came in, we went out. From the Italian runways to the French fashion scene to the catwalks in New York, there is a worldwide trend to exclude black models from fashion shows. Only a few shows for the fall 1996 season included a black face, and even then in several cases that face could have been mistaken for white. Magazines and newspapers – many of which use pictures from runway shows throughout the year – had few chances to include us in their pages. We are seldom the focal point of the main fashion layouts in general market publications.

'Clearly the black model is the subject of a damaging and demeaning disappearing act. During these lean seasons for sisters, I wonder what will become of the current crop of up-and-coming black models trying to make the leap to supermodel. The new bevy of black beauties includes Lorraine Pascale, whose close-cropped coif, half-moon smile and African features landed her an *Elle* cover.' This makes Lorraine's regular appearances all the more remarkable. She was also to be one of several black models to appear on the cover or on the pages of *Sports Illustrated* over the years. Others included Jessica White, Roshumba Williams and Carla Campbell. (Tyra Banks was the first black model to grace the front cover in 1996.)

One particularly striking image of Lorraine with her shaved head during this period appeared in fashion magazine *Mirabella*. The mono picture, taken by noted photographer Stephanie Pfriender Stylander, was called 'Urban White' and orchestrated by fashion director Polly Hamilton and Sam Shahid. It featured Lorraine wearing a white jacket with her face reflected in a glass building. In true photo speak Stylander described the picture thus: 'My objective was to pair beautiful architectural locations with elements of strong graphic lines, with Lorraine being equal to the power of the space. The choice of the potent yellow color of the night light and the use of black and white imagery created an interesting juxtaposition.'

Lorraine also made appearances in the British edition of *Elle* in November 1990 in a 'Velvet Underground' shoot by Mario Testino and in December 1991 in an 'Urban Softwear' shoot ('Soften this winter's slick of PVC with sumptuous mohair sweaters'), *The Face* in February 1991 standing alongside Kate Moss on an empty road in a 'Heaven is Real' shoot by top photographer the late Corinne Day (there are still some unpublished pictures from the shoot around), in which Day is said to have 'evoked the power of female friendship,' adding: 'Through the sequence of images Kate Moss and Lorraine Pascale appear carefree and exuberant at one moment and hesitant the next' – and another Corinne Day shoot, 'Borneo', in August 1991 – again with Kate Moss.

Corinne Day died of cancer at the age of just 48 in 2010 and these photographs were amongst a collection that went on show honouring her work. They also appear in the book *Heaven is Real*, published by Morel.

Lorraine was also photographed by Thierry Le Goués for an eye-catching set of images in the December 1991/February 1992 issue of France's *Vogue Hommes* magazine, in which she wore 'street entertainer' clothes (in one she poses as a fire-eater). There was also *Harper's Bazaar* in February 1993 ('Let It rain, The Fashion Forecast for Raincoats – Airy, Lightweight, Breezy to Throw Over Anything. You Don't Have to Wait for the Downpour') when she was photographed wearing a bright yellow, full-length coat alongside a yellow taxi, a full-length black coat and a black shiny mac alongside another up-and-coming supermodel Naomi Campbell. Lorraine appeared again in March of that year in a 'Rags to Riches' shoot in the middle of two other black models, Brandi Quinones and Beverly Peele. Lorraine looked particularly gorgeous in the pale, romantic dresses of the fashion spread with the words 'when evening dances a fine line between dress and undress'. Both shoots were by Peter Lindbergh.

She wore a black dress with a transparent skirt and black stockings for a Patrick Demarchelier shoot, also in 1993 for *Harper's*, and was in the magazine again in May 1994 for a 'Taking Off' shoot and in August the same year in a 'Stealing the Show' spread. In November 1994 Lorraine was one of a group of beautiful girls in a Primo Prada shoot by Bruce Weber for US *Vogue*. She was back in *Harper's Bazaar* in February 1997 in a 'Health: Energy' feature.

Sports Illustrated Swimwear magazine of 1998 saw Lorraine in a shoot with Heidi Klum and Tyra Banks. There were five pictures of Lorraine: one lying down topless but with her arm across her breasts. She wore swimsuits of vibrant orange and pink, which created a striking affect with her dark skin and dramatically short hair. The shoot was, she said, 'a major deal'. It also presented the opportunity of visiting Ecuador and spending ten days on a trimaran sailing around the Galapagos Islands.

Modelling sounds like an idyllic lifestyle, but things didn't always go well. Once, when Lorraine was in Senegal on a shoot for *Marie Claire* magazine, she awoke one morning with a face 'the size of a football' staring back at her in the mirror. She had been bitten all over (probably by mosquitoes) including around her eyes and on her nose. A total disaster for a model on such a prestigious job! And no pictures had yet been taken. The shoot still went ahead but Lorraine had to wear sunglasses and a deliberate, slightly out-of-focus series of photographs were called for.

But Lorraine was also getting mentions in less glossy publications. She had a name check in Jamaica's *Kingston Gleaner* newspaper in November 1994 under the headline 'Young Models Making Waves', which described how 'currently a wave of black British models including Lorraine Pascale have been invading the US' and were following 'a path opened by pioneering Naomi Campbell who's now the top paid black model.' But in support of its local models and in criticism of the fashion industry's fight to get girls to the top, it added: 'The industry has been one of pitting models against each other as if there is only room for one at the top.'

Lorraine's regular assignments all came her way by not existing on a model's diet – for most of the time. Back then, she says, models actually ate. Neither was there the call for 'heroin chic', with models then being a healthy size eight or ten – 'slightly more do-able than the required size six or four today. We were slim not skinny, so even then I ate properly.' (Lorraine has said people cannot believe a former model would make a career out of food. She has been asked so many times about why she gave up modelling that she now makes the joke 'Because I was hungry!') However, Lorraine has admitted that there were times when she did indeed have to watch her eating habits. She insists there was no starving or dieting but in the run-up to an underwear or swimsuit shoot, throughout the week before she would perhaps 'eat a little less'. But she is at pains to point out that at the time she started modelling – the late 80s – 'the girls looked very different. We all ate normally, so food was always there. Fashion samples were a 10–12; models were curvaceous and athletic like Cindy Crawford. They looked healthy in a way that might be seen as "too fat" for fashion now.' That meant although she and the other models who shared a flat were careful about what they ate – 'I was mindful of what I put in my mouth' – they still occasionally bought family buckets of Kentucky Fried Chicken 'to take home and stuff ourselves with'.

There was also the high-flying world of the catwalk: Betty Jackson in 1992 at which Lorraine cut a striking figure with her savage crop and wearing a long black coat), John Galliano's spring/summer collection in

1993; Chanel's and Hermès' autumn/winter show of 1994 and a haute couture showing of Christian Lacroix that same year; two Chanels in 1995 (there is a video clip still available of Lorraine strutting her stuff on the catwalk) and an Alexander McQueen collection the following year.

Watching Lorraine's career take off one might easily have construed her as being fiercely ambitious when it came to modelling. Not so. For Lorraine it was simply a case of 'putting one foot in front of the other' – that and wearing 'the shortest skirts and five-inch heels'. She was happy enough to allow designers to put her in the clothes they chose. There were also the perks. After one fashion show Lorraine was given 15 pairs of Karl Lagerfeld shoes. So there was the glamour and the fame and the gifts. But Lorraine has admitted that because of her youth and having a 'lot of front' it didn't seem a big deal at the time, though she did love modelling – perks and pitfalls, successes and insecurities included. 'I learned that it's important to do a job you love! And how insecure women are. People assume that because these girls are gorgeous, everything's all fine but it's not. No one's going to pity models for this, but when you've only been judged on your looks and nothing else, you wonder if people really like you for who you are. So it can be empty. It wasn't always what was wanted.' During her 17-year modelling career Lorraine was used in several advertising campaigns including Donna Karan, Rive Gauche, Hermès, Versace (with one appearance in *Detour* magazine with her name spelled 'Pascal' in March 1995 when her already dramatic look was heightened by heavy black make-up encircling her eyes), Yves Saint Laurent, Nick Coleman, Gap (in one of her most casual looks of jeans and T-shirt) and Banana Republic. The 1993 campaign for New York store Barneys saw Lorraine smiling, bare-footed and wearing a pale-blue skirt just above the knee and a matching long pale-blue jacket. The advertising photograph (taken by Corinne Day) was accompanied by a rather obscure caption: 'Simplicity: Cross out half of what you write. Don't say half of what you think. Get rid of half your clothes, furniture and friends. Answer questions true or false. Look on the bright side and if there isn't one buy a flashlight.'

There was also a somewhat raunchy 1991 'Lose Control' advertising campaign for luxury ice cream brand Häagen-Dazs in which Lorraine, dressed in a cropped white sports top and white knickers, appeared to be force feeding a rather good-looking white man (topless of course) with a tub of the ice cream. This prompted Marion Humes, writing for the *Independent* in an article about models featuring in advertising campaigns, to say: 'If the British model Lorraine Pascale consumes Häagen-Dazs with the abandon suggested by her ad, she must have a dynamic metabolism.' It might just have been another model job for Lorraine, but the whole Häagen-Dazs advertising campaign tactic was seen as much more than that by professional observers. One critique by Gender Studies said the words signified 'a sexual innuendo (together with the photo of a couple in underwear and in an intimate, playful embrace to the right) where buyers are encouraged to "lose control" both by eating ice cream and presumably by having amazing sex.'

One of Lorraine's first pieces of publicity came in September 1993 in the first-ever issue of the American magazine *Vibe*, 'the first mass-market magazine to follow hip-hop and urban music and culture'. It is worth quoting the article in full, not only for its American hip style of writing, but also because it highlights the rarity of black models at the time, including references to actor/model Jason Olive and stunning cover girl Karen Alexander. There is also mention of Lorraine's striking sheared haircut – and one of her rare admissions that she hoped to make her mark in acting and singing as well as modelling:

'That's right y'all. Lorraine Pascale is B-L-A-C-K. If you're like most Nubians or Europeans who have no use for yellow Africans it's predictable protocol that the espresso complexion just got you wide open. If you're like my Grandma who cringes at the sight of full lips, nappy hair and coffee-without-milk colored skin you probably would have mistaken the beauty for sweetness or intelligence had it been seated in your living room. And if you're like me whose Grandma encouraged her to stay smart and sweet, you smile every time you see Lorraine Pascale's face. Revenge couldn't be sweeter than a full-lipped, bald-headed, blue-black model rakin' in the modelling dough. But even fiercer is the fact that every time Pascale appears in magazines and advertisements her image reeks of Afro-Caribbean diva attitude. Although she was born to Jamaican and St Lucian parents Lorraine was adopted and raised by white folks in London. "It's strange," Pascale says with a smile (the black sensibility) "must be there on a subconscious level." If you've ever eyed African models you know that they can either project their black-girl flavor or pose in blackface. While Pascale has chosen the former, doing so hasn't been the easiest task. "In the beginning," – she pauses – "it used to really get to me." Late last year with center parts and shags being "in"– and modelling paying the bills – Lorraine traded her natural for a weave. "But then all of the sudden I didn't care," she says with a giggle. "I'm black. I'm African. And I'm strong. I don't want to sit in a chair six hours every three months to get these things put in my hair and pay all this money. This is me. If you don't like it then don't book me. If you want somebody with bone-straighter hair then book a white girl." Angry letters protesting Banana Republic's booking of one too many white girls is how she and Jason Olive wound up in the clothier's spring ad campaign. Like the booking of Karen Alexander by Ralph "Polo" Lauren a few years back this is a tremendous milestone in Pascale's career. Regardless, she knows that most advertisers still consider "black girls' features too strong". Case in point is the current retro-70s waif bandwagon which has not provided much work for black models. Pascale says: "As far as the industry is concerned, there aren't any black girls." But rather than let the politics overwhelm her Pascale has learned to use them to her advantage. Not only is she guaranteed most of the work in the ethnic casting (see Barneys New York 1993 spring campaign, *Allure* and *Bazaar*) but she gets to travel and make more money than the average 20-year-old. Pascale's three-year-old gig is merely a stepping stone to the next point – acting and singing. "Once I've reached the top there," she says with a smile, "Then I'll be on the cover of *Bazaar* and *Vogue*."'

The article was accompanied by a black and white photograph of Lorraine blowing copious amounts of cigarette smoke.

So, proving those agents from the days of begging to be taken on so wrong, Lorraine's look was one that worked well for both edgy and classic campaigns. With her ability to move from sultry to smiley, chic to cheek, she was in great demand. Already there at the top, she was famous enough to appear in an airline magazine article 'Famous Frequent Fliers' revealing what she carried in her suitcase – a 'small, black canvas Mandarina Duck holdall' and its contents – 'a bottle of mineral water and herbal drops'. (Nowadays, Lorraine's iPhone, loaded with books to catch up on, and headphones so she can listen to music while exercising – yes, even on holiday – will always travel with her.)

Lorraine was working with all the leading photographers – and then came the chance to work with the photographer of the moment, Steven Meisel. 'I thought, "Oh my God, I can't be working for him!"' she recalled of the time when she heard who would be taking the pictures. American photographer Meisel really was the one all the models wanted to work with. By the time he was introduced to Lorraine he had a strong pedigree. One young Kate Moss was his protégée. He also helped launch the career of Linda Evangelista.

It was the time of top money for top models who were cashing in with cosmetics companies. One of the 'top five', Claudia Schiffer, was paid a reported $8.5m

(£5.3m) for a four-year contract with Revlon. Then there were the big demands for walking along the catwalks with models paid anything from $10,000 (£6,200) to $35,000 (£21,800) per appearance at the big shows. But Lorraine must have had a bit of struggle on her hands to convince Meisel she had the right look, for he decried how in the late 80s 'the Amazon woman' image had taken over. 'We were brainwashed into seeing qualities like gentleness and sensitive as negative and weak,' said Meisel, who, in 1992 had bemoaned the fact that models no longer looked 'innocent' but 'aggressive and tough'.

So it was with a rather cynical Meisel that Lorraine had to pose in the lucrative Iceberg designer clothing campaign several years later in 1996. One shot was of her in a dark satin jacket, silver shorts and white high-heeled shoes. She was certainly of Amazon stature. And her short hair (now long enough to be slicked back) certainly gave her a rather tough image. But any discussion about the rights and wrongs as seen by the fickle fashion industry did not concern her at the time. She admitted she simply took the money and ran – or most probably gracefully strode away at least. And even at the tender age of 19, she knew that she would give up the business before it gave up on her. 'It is easy money. It doesn't last all that long, so you might as well milk the business while you can,' she confessed. 'I can't see myself doing it for a long time.'

And though still only young, Lorraine was astute enough to know that she was simply a clothes horse in the eyes of designers and photographers. She said: 'It's fun sometimes, but it can also be really degrading. And it's not as exciting as the magazines and newspapers make out. No one is really interested in your opinion. It's a case of "here's a size eight dress and size six shoes. It doesn't matter if they don't fit, just put them on and be quiet."' It was therefore not the most compatible of careers for Lorraine, who said simply: 'I wanted to use my brain.' In the same, rare interview with *Sunday Age* she first expressed her desire to go into acting, admitting that was probably because she had got used to 'getting attention'. There were a few occasions when Lorraine made it on film. She appeared as a 'Bond girl' around the roulette table at a casino in Robbie Williams' video for the song 'Millennium' from his 1998 *I've Been Expecting You* album and is glimpsed several times. Now, if we've got it right, Lorraine is one of the girls dressed in a gold evening dress who at one point lies pretty close to Robbie in his self-confessed spoof James Bond role; she even strokes his arm. This didn't seem enough for him as he commented afterwards: 'It was my chance to have girls y'know fawning over me, but like paying 'em which is something I haven't done ever before in private. The models on the shoot, cause I knew a couple of them, and they weren't fawning enough, in fact they were a bit like bored of the whole day, and they didn't fawn enough. And I remember phoning them up or speaking to them the next day and saying "Look, this is my video shoot, this is my dream. I'm paying you, you fawn a lot bigger and a lot better than that, whether you fancy me or not!"'

With or without the fawning, the video did help Robbie to have his first number one of that year. And if you don't blink, you will see Lorraine providing a very easy-on-the-eye companion for him. In the not-too-wonderful 1992 movie *Split Second* Lorraine is credited as 'girl in nightclub' under her full name Lorraine Pascale Woodward. The film, starring Rutger Hauer and Kim Cattrall, is set in futuristic London where rising sea levels mean that large areas of the city are under water. Hauer plays a cop who previously lost his partner to a strange creature. Now the creature is back and it's after him.

Lorraine was also an extra in the 2001 film *Blow Dry*, listed as Lorraine Balinska (more about that name later), taking the part of Ebony, a hairdresser. Fellow supermodel Heidi Klum was hairdresser Jasmine. The main stars were Natasha Richardson and Alan Rickman and the story told of how the town of Keighley hosts the British annual hairdressing championship and how it affects certain local people. Though by no means starring roles, Lorraine did credit a mention in *Screen World* (vol 53) in 2002 and she was on the list of those attending the premiere of *Blow Dry*. She was also a fully paid up member of Equity, though the BECS (British Equity Collecting Society) nowadays has Lorraine Pascale-Woodward as one of their 'missing performers' – one of those with whom they had lost contact.

Lorraine soon realised that not only was an acting career not for her but deep down the whole glamour thing wasn't either. It was never meant to be 'forever' she has said. Modelling assignments meant all that waiting around – the boredom, the not being allowed to express an opinion, the merely being treated as a silent clothes horse. Her comment bears repeating: 'People assume that because these girls are gorgeous, everything's fine, but it's not. No one's going to pity models for this, but when you've only been judged on your looks and nothing else, you wonder if people really like you for who you are. So it can be empty.'

Despite her success, Lorraine was beginning to regret her decision to leave school so early and reiterated her belief: 'I also think that 16 is too young to start modelling. At that age you need to get an education.' But this was not as straightforward for Lorraine as it might be for most children. Her moves from one family to another also meant a change of school and the accompanying disruption in her education. Lorraine feels this affected her learning and she is still conscious that there were important subjects she did not master as well as she could have – 'I missed out on English grammar because I was always moving schools – you need to learn social skills and how to be an adult. I'm not sure how much you grow up, modelling.' But she has made the poignant point that for her, modelling made her feel like she belonged and that there were people looking out for her. 'You're very looked after. At the time I thought I'd built up this other family, but it's a very fractured experience. You get very close to people on a job, and then maybe don't see them again for a year. I loved it, but it wasn't what I needed long-term.'

Fortunately for Lorraine her real family remained in the background to ensure the modelling mayhem and madness did not go to her head. It was they who, when Lorraine returned from a modelling trip with its private cars and flights in the then supersonic Concorde, brought the girl whose younger days were spent in a housing association back down to earth. For even Lorraine, as cynical as she was about the modelling world, had to admit that models were 'actual celebrities' and recognised wherever they went. 'It was amazing; incredibly glamorous. New York in the heyday with Naomi and Cindy and Linda at every show; limousines waiting to pick you up. Mobile phones before anyone else had them.' Her family kept her grounded. 'They would tell me it was my turn to put the rubbish out!' she once admitted. She has also said that although she was pleased for the likes of Naomi Campbell, who was making vast sums at the time, the supermodel 'should remember where she came from' before adding: 'It's important to have good friends back at home otherwise you could turn into something you're not.'

There were times too when Lorraine wanted to break out on shoots and display her natural exuberance. But it was difficult sometimes to present a dark, sombre look when she felt so bubbly inside. The brooding image wasn't always easy to project for the camera. And on occasions she was desperate to present her fun side – though mixed in with the sultry pictures are lots of her smiling, winking and stretching those lovely long limbs. She said: 'I did struggle because I wanted to talk to people and be lively and they just didn't understand it. I was quite a smiley model. There are pictures of me leaping around, and they just didn't understand it.' Not being able to be herself was another reason why Lorraine decided to leave the modelling limelight. The not being understood was, she said, 'when I started soul-searching for something else'.

But all in all, Lorraine has said she was 'incredibly lucky' to be a model. 'The travel and money was great, but it is harder work than a lot people realise and it can be quite a lonely job at times. It's better than working in a factory, though, so I'll always be grateful.' There was also someone in the background giving Lorraine inspiration. Her father – 'Popsicle' – has always been a great mentor to her and Lorraine wanted to find the kind of work satisfaction that he himself had experienced as a college lecturer. 'My father is a very intelligent man and every morning when he woke up he was so excited about going to work. He had a passion and I wanted that.' She still feels that she was very much a model 'by default' and that she kind of fell into the career rather than made a positive choice about it.

Lorraine has not entirely forgotten her modelling days, though. On her official website she has a selection of her favourite pictures. She has captioned them 'Fabulous in Fur', 'Fashionably Late' (with a back shot of her on the steps of an apartment), 'A Winning Camio Combo', and 'Rock 'n' Romantic' for a fashion spread. There is also a stunning picture of her in a long red dress with a white edge holding baby Ella, who is wrapped in a matching shawl.

Chapter 4

Countess Lorraine

In 1995, while in America and at the age of 23, Lorraine had married Kaz Balinski-Jundzill. Daughter Ella was born a year later, in November 1996. Lorraine had come back to Britain for the birth – which like that of Ella's father was registered as having taken place in Westminster. Which brings us to the colourful background of Lorraine's former husband. In newspaper and magazine articles he has always been referred to somewhat dismissively as a 'Polish musician'. He has been described as Count Kaz, the 'Count' often put in quote marks as if it is a rather grand stage name – think American jazz pianist William 'Count Basie' – and hence he is often referred to as 'Polish musician, "Count" Kaz Balinski-Jundzill'. This rather understates his true background – and current status. He is a very wealthy businessman with interesting historical links. And he has indeed inherited the aristocratic title. Balinski-Jundzill's true profile has never been previously revealed in relation to his marriage to Lorraine, and she quite understandably has not volunteered much detail about the man who was to treat her so badly. But it makes fascinating reading – and in turn, had a much greater impact on Lorraine's life than has previously been reported.

Kaz Balinski-Jundzill was born in 1968, the second son, and bearing the full name Kazimierz (sometimes Kazimierez), of Count Chris Balinski-Jundzill and Katrina Mary Emmott. His brother is Zygmunt, often called Ziggy or Zygi. Katrina (née Rycroft) was the daughter of Mary and John Bingham Emmott (whose father, Yorkshireman Willie, had made his fortune from a company called Automotive Products – and was, incidentally, to live to the ripe old age of 100). Lorraine still uses the name 'Emmott' as part of the Balinski-Jundzill name and daughter Ella sometimes uses it – though her birth is actually registered as Ella Pascale Balinska. The family's Polish heritage is worth a mention. Count Chris's father – Kaz's grandfather – was Count Jan Balinski-Jundzill, who was born in Poland in 1899. Between 1930 and 1939 he was president of Catholic Action in eastern Poland, but his family fled the country when the Red Army invaded in 1939. They found refuge in Britain with friends Balinski-Jundzill had made during his time as president of the International Student Movement. During his time in Britain Balinski-Jundzill held many Catholic-related posts. He was also a member of the Polish government, serving the Polish Research Centre during the Second World War, and such was his reverence, when he died in 1974 a Requiem Mass was held at Westminster Cathedral.

The marriage of Katrina and Count Chris Balinski-Jundzill did not last and Katrina went to live in County Wicklow, Ireland (one assumes she took her sons with her and that it was here that one of the family seats was established – of which more later). Katrina's ex-husband lives in America. Kaz showed an early interest in music – hence the 'Polish musician' tag – and went on to form a band The Rocketeers (not to be confused with current bands of the same name). His fellow band member was West End actor Mike Dyer (who nowadays describes himself as 'producer, concept writer and composer').

Though few film clips of them still exist, there is one – 'A Kaz Balinski Show' – showing them behaving rather badly in Henley-on-Thames, back in 1990. The 32-year-old Kaz, with hair past his shoulders and dressed in a somewhat foppish hat and coat, and Dyer set off homemade fireworks in a terrifying display that ended with the arrival of the police. Kaz introduces himself as 'Kaz Balinski, Rocketeer'. The clip features blonde Mary Bird, who also had music connections, having sung with 'The Stiff All-Stars' a group signed up to Stiff Records, and who introduces the 'Rocketeers of Henley'.

Balinski – or rather *Count* Balinski – was still greatly in hippy mode when he married Lorraine. As two of New York's socialites, they were photographed in their New York apartment, which Lorraine later titled 'Rocking with Count Balinski'. The pair present a startling contrast. Lorraine has her shaven head and is wearing a white vest top, shorts and perilously high black heels. It is she who is posing with a guitar, while then fiancé Balinski, with hair not far off waist-length, bare-footed, bare-chested and wearing a crushed velvet maroon suit, looks on. On the wall of the apartment is a dramatic painting titled 'The Gladiator' by renowned British artist Julian Opie.

Balinski seems to have made some contribution to the music industry – though not perhaps in the way he might have wished – having linked up with Pete Cornish, 'creator of integrated guitar affects and amp routing systems for the world's best-known performers'. Cornish specialises in selling high-specification musical equipment and in 1993 and 1994 alongside Paul McCartney, Dave Gilmour and

Lou Reed, who were giving fellow musicians the chance to buy their equipment, Kaz was offering his 24-track digital recording system, guitar effects board and 24-channel keyboard instrument for sale.

It has been reported that Lorraine and Kaz Balinski divorced in 2001. (American state law for New York does not allow marriage and divorce records to be made public.) But Lorraine, whose decision it was to end the marriage, actually got the papers for her decree nisi in October 1999 – according to a presumably accurate report in the Nigel Dempster diary column of the *Daily Mail* at the time. The decree absolute normally follows within six weeks, making the end of the marriage final. However, in Lorraine's case there could have been reasons for the delay. As the Law Practice states: 'The reason that so many divorcees appear to experience such a long wait for their divorces to come through is that this is rarely applied for until all thorny matters between the petitioner and respondent have been settled – matters of child and/or pet custody, property and financial affairs. Any divorce lawyers worth their salt will strongly advise their clients not to apply for the decree absolute until absolutely all of these matters have been taken care of.' This could well have been the case with Lorraine considering the rather complex finances of the Balinski-Jundzill family. It was also not a straightforward separation. Lorraine cited her husband's adultery as grounds for divorce so it is likely the whole business would have been somewhat acrimonious.

One wonders if this has anything to do with the fact that while she was having to deal with his unfaithfulness, the ending of her marriage and all the accompanying despair, the 'other woman' was already preparing to take her place. Interior designer Vanessa Hart made a formal application to change her name to Balinska-Jundzill (Balinski and Balinska are regularly varied in the family) by deed poll in October 2000. This seems somewhat indecent haste, given that Lorraine's divorce was reportedly not finalised until a year later. There is also the question why Hart and Balinski did not wait until he was free and then marry.

Lorraine's replacement actually had her official name change agreed on 18 October 2000, with it being formally endorsed on 26 October at the Supreme Court of Judicature (encompassing the Court of Appeal, the High Court of Justice and the Crown Court). An announcement in the 'Changes of Name' section of the *London Gazette* appeared on 27 November. And so it was – with no marriage mentioned – that Vanessa Mariam Hart was now to be legally known as Vanessa Mariam Balinska-Jundzill. Her address was given as a flat in Buckingham Palace Road, southwest London and she was referred to as 'single' and a 'British citizen'. She had, the notice said, 'abandoned the surname of Hart' and assumed that of Balinska-Jundzill.

Acting for Vanessa Hart was law firm Farrer & Co – notably solicitors to HM The Queen and who represented Prince Charles in his divorce from Princess Diana of 1996 (her final settlement was estimated at £17m but she had to relinquish her Royal Highness title). It seems though, in Vanessa's case the firm helped her gain a title – she is referred to as Countess Balinska-Jundzill in relation to some of the family's companies (although she is known simply as Vanessa Balinska at the British Institute of Interior Design). This all adds up to a bit of a thorny problem, as will be seen later.

It is no wonder that Lorraine has since been so guarded about commitment and relationships. The failure of her marriage had a traumatic effect on her. Over the course of a few months the stress turned her ebony coloured hair grey. She made a trip to Boots 'and bought whatever was on the shelf in jet black. I don't think I'd look good with a big white Afro!' Lorraine later returned to Britain and found a new home in Battersea. She was now a single mother but she was financially stable. Obviously her divorce was a sad and dramatic event, but she did not face the financial problems many in her position have to deal with. There was the cushion of money saved from her modelling which later enabled her to buy a flat in

Chelsea, where she still lives, and the settlement from her marriage. Interestingly, Lorraine's two companies, Mint and Lime Limited and Cupcake Bakehouse Limited, are registered in the name of Lorraine Balinski-Jundzill at Burnham-on-Sea in Somerset. (Her very first company, Glutilicious Limited, registered under the same name is now dissolved.) She is also still listed under that name as the director of a property management team, Towncraft Limited, having been appointed to that position in February 2002, not long after her divorce, although the company was registered in 1985. Her occupation is described as being 'of independent means'. Towncraft's current financial situation in 2012 was not wildly promising, with its value given as a token £2 following submission of accounts.

In turn, Kaz and his brother are described as having 'many business interests' including information technology and entertainment. But then Kaz is a wealthy man in his own right. Following the divorce Lorraine gave herself a two-year breathing space to work out 'what made me tick'. In a bid to provide her daughter with the early chances she herself had never had, Lorraine enrolled Ella in an independent school. Lorraine 'showered' Ella 'with love' – something she knows only too well is the most important thing you can give a child – together with security, the one thing she herself never had. Lorraine has said she is happy to have had a child when she was young, even though marriage was 'a bit of a gamble'.

Meanwhile, as Lorraine was getting her life back together, her ex-husband, today director of several companies, was promoting one of them. He was sponsoring the 2002 50th British Water Ski tournament nationals at Princes Club, Bedfont in Middlesex – well, his 'new and exciting energy drink' called 'Spiked Silver' was doing so, via his company, Silver Arrow Establishment. Not one to miss a chance, Balinski extolled the virtues of his product: 'We're delighted to be able to help the British National Tournament in this way. Water-skiing is a great sport and one that I'm personally very passionate about. If we can help attract more people or media attention to the tournament through sponsorship, that would make us really proud. Our product – Spiked Silver cranberry energy drink – is aimed at young, energetic and fun people with impeccable taste, so it's certainly a great synergy for us. Good luck from all of us to everyone competing!'

Balinski's Silver Arrow Establishment is still in existence. So too is his company Grand Prix '6' Ltd. For seven years too, from 2002 Balinski was a director at a company called Provider, based in Duane Street, New York. Provider is owned by the hugely successful group Related, a privately owned real estate firm, and according to its website boasts a 'high premier portfolio of high quality assets valued at over $12b'. Balinski left in 2009. He later became involved with another New York company. Five other companies he has been involved with – and which were mainly to do with the music and entertainment business – have since been dissolved.

Lorraine's marriage might have been a gamble yes, certainly on the emotional and personal side. But it is presumed that a financial settlement was to cushion the cost of building a new life and career. It also greatly enhanced the connections of the woman everyone knows as the model-turned-chef Lorraine Pascale. Having been married to a Count qualified her to be called Countess. It all gets a bit muddled here as she sometimes uses the name Countess Lorraine Balinska – not Balinski. Indeed she appeared on TV as Countess Lorraine Balinska on 2 July 2008, three years before she hit our television screens with her first TV series.

So what was this appearance all about? Lorraine was one of 200 people who converged on a barn in West Sussex to sample an all-British menu harvested and literally hunted by British chef and restaurateur Marco Pierre White (the man who was to encourage her to bake for Selfridges that same year). The event was filmed for the Marco Pierre White *Great British Feast* programme on ITV. While Pierre White was 'working flat out to get everything ready on time',

Lorraine and her fellow diners were on their way. They were, we were told: 'Diners from all corners of the British Isles'. Lorraine was interviewed on camera under the credit 'Countess Lorraine Balinska, pastry chef'. She was, she said, 'expecting to eat a lot, expecting to adjust the belt on my jeans' and generally enjoy the feast, adding: 'I like the idea of hunting and serving food. It is back to basics.' Lorraine later proclaimed the smoked eel as 'Very tasty, very fresh; perfectly seasoned. Heavenly!' While on the Countess link, it is interesting to note that one of Lorraine's favourite chefs is American Ina Garten – known as 'The Barefoot Contessa'. What is even more intriguing is that there seem to be two Countess Balinskas – Countess Lorraine and Countess Vanessa – both through association with the same man.

Despite the split, Ella's father is still involved in her life and the two are very close. Ella spends regular time with him at his home in Ireland where he lives with Vanessa, whom he has described as 'a hot, loving wife' who is 'pretty patient too'. He also gives praise to his 'lovely children'. But Ella's trips to see her father are far removed from those of most other girls visiting their dads for a rather mundane weekend of trips to a fast food outlet or the park. In fact, Ella has her very own, rather large park. Kaz Balinski's family own Glendalough Estate in Annamoe, County Wicklow.

The 1,500-acre estate, about 25 miles from Dublin, is glowingly described as made up of 'mountainside, woodlands, pastures, rolling parklands and historic buildings situated in the heart of Wicklow, Ireland's Garden County'. Oh, and we must not forget the historic and exotic 12-acre Water Garden and the fact that the grounds have thrown up some of the oldest archaeological finds in Ireland. In short, Glendalough House is hailed as one of Ireland's most important historic sites.

Today, the grand house and its grounds hosts hospitality and sporting events and 'entertainment solutions to individuals, groups and parties looking for adventure, exploration and escape in a private, idyllic, yet dedicated setting'. It is no wonder that the location is used for many film and TV shoots – *Kidnapped* and *Excalibur* are just two. In 2010 the location also hosted the Irish Green Gathering Festival with around 5,000 people and more than 100 stalls. The main purpose of the event was to 'bring environmental and sustainable living and to put on the festival in a sustainable manner' with 'everything that can be recycled at the event is recycled... every plate, fork, spoon, knife, cup, bowl, napkin, coffee stirrer and sample cup is 100% biodegradable and will be collected with all food scraps to be composted.' Kaz Balinski, described as 'a successful businessman in his own right', is credited for being committed to turning the area into a permanent festival site and home for the Irish Green Gathering.

The estate is also an equestrian centre. But it was Balinski himself who came up with the idea of turning part of the estate into a mountain-bike park, a dream fulfilled in 2012. One event alone attracted nearly 300 bikers from all over the country. An enthusiastic biker himself, Balinski is often seen roaring around the track. His love of bikes came at an early age and he had some illustrious company even as a child. Kaz gets an honorary mention in *Long Way Round: Chasing Shadows Across the World*, a book written by actor Ewan McGregor and 'TV adventurer', actor and writer Charley Boorman. In it, Boorman recalls how, as a neighbour of the Balinskis in County Wicklow, he teamed up with Kaz for racing fun as a child. 'By the time I was 12 I got to know Kaz Balinski who lived across from our farm. Kaz, who had a Yamaha YZ-801, had built a motocross track. We would race our bikes down to the bottom of my parents' fields, through the river into the Balinskis' field and up the hill to Kaz's motocross track, where we would bounce around the circuit, racing, tumbling and falling until it got dark.'

Lorraine is sanguine about her marriage: she believes her young age was one of the reasons why it failed. That and her conflicting desire to feel wanted and secure while always finding it hard to trust someone. In this case, it seems her insecurity was not misplaced, with her husband having an affair – 'I got married very quickly, divorced very quickly. Back to where I was before…' With her tumultuous background, the stress of trying to find a permanent haven while always waiting for it to end is perhaps understandable. Lorraine told *The Times*: 'Obviously I trust everyday things but to have deep trust is very difficult. For most children, even if your mum and dad are a pain in the arse and there are arguments and they annoy you, you still know that they're there. If you haven't had that constant security with your parents, you're going to doubt it when you meet someone.'

There have been other men in Lorraine's life before she met her current – and likely long-term – partner Ged Doherty, though. In August 1999 Lorraine was linked with 44-year-old property developer Christopher Whalley, once an escort of the late Princess Diana – who incidentally introduced herself to him at her regular gym the Harbour Club, with the words: 'What does a girl have to do to get a coffee around here?' While the chat-up line between Whalley and Lorraine is not recorded, Whalley, who had come out of a relationship with fashion designer Amanda Wakeley, did admit they had met at that very same Harbour Club. Speaking at new jazz restaurant Brompton Bay, Whalley said: 'We're together but have not known each other for very long.'

By then, Lorraine had already separated fro.
Balinski so their marriage was actually well and truly
over well before their divorce. The relationship with
Whalley was not to last, though, and forming long-
term partnerships was still a challenge for Lorraine.
But now in what happily appears to be a forever
relationship with Doherty, she feels secure. She has
said: 'I have worked through it now, but I used to go
out with someone and the minute something went
wrong, I'd just be like, "Right, I'm out." I'd panic
rather than work through it.'

Chapter 5

Cooking up a career

It was in 2000, a year or so after separating from her husband, that Lorraine decided to give up modelling full-time – one reason being to spend more time with Ella. Of course it was also a tumultuous year for Lorraine whose termination of her marriage was further marred by Balinski's decision to start a new life with Vanessa Hart. With reference to her determination to do what she felt was right, Lorraine said: 'As a child I was always taught that I could do anything I put my mind to as long as I tried hard enough, so I guess that became my mantra and after a while I was pretty miserable modelling so wanted a change and also wanted to be with my daughter rather than flying around all the time.'

But she was still taking on modelling jobs in between trying to find a new career for herself. And there have been 'comebacks'. Lorraine was on the catwalk during America's Fashion Week of 2009, modelling Aquascutum's 'winter/fall collection'. It was an event which once again raised the issue of the use of black models. Reporting on America's *Jezebel* magazine website in February of that year under the headline 'Will The Credit Crunch Mean Fewer Black Models?' Dodai Stewart rather strangely links this with the 'recession', a claim apparently backed up by Carol White of Premier Model Management, who said: 'In a time of recession, people want to play it safe with blonde-haired, blue-eyed girls. It's very much the case at the moment that everyone plays it safe and I think it will get worse in the recession. People don't step out of line.'

Commented Stewart: 'Hear that? Hiring models of color is stepping out of line. Breaking the "rules." And if you do it? You're fucking with your money. Of course, fashion is a business. And fashion is about exclusivity. But in this day and age, can companies really afford to exclude a certain percentage of the population? Or appear to do so?'

A spokesperson for Lorraine's agency Storm, begged to differ, listing models who didn't fit the blonde, blue-eyed mould. 'We're finding that clients are looking for girls who are a little bit different and interesting. Our black girls did brilliantly in London Fashion Week. People like Alek Wek, Jourdan Dunn and Lorraine Pascale were booked for lots of shows.'

None of the ongoing debate about black models in the industry held Lorraine back, even in her later years, however. In May 2010 she was on the list of '40 Hottest Black Beauties that Made the Fashion Scene Tremble' compiled by website The Fashionables. For those who made it on to the list, the tribute was glowing: 'The beauty of African American women is something so notorious that the fashion world could not have escaped it. Ebony beauties with feline bodies have conquered the fashion catwalk and the covers of fashion and style magazines. What exactly makes them unique? In order to answer that question one should consider that the exquisite charm of these amazing black beauties is absolutely singular. They have the air of the Queen of Sheba and in the same time all the exotic appeal of a modern statue. The black models have entered the fashion world with all the wild charm of their race and made a stand becoming true images of glamor that shook up a bit what the society considered beauty standards before them. Here are 40 amazing beauties that made a name for black fashion models.'

Lorraine's eternal appeal also saw her as the first black cover girl in the 125-year history of *The Lady* magazine in February 2011 – 'Scrumptious! From

Catwalk to Kitchen, baking beauty Lorraine Pascale'. Inside were a couple of Lorraine's recipes and Carolyn Hart wrote glowingly of how 'Indeed, Pascale is pretty spectacular looking herself, which must account for some of her popularity. You mean, "we, too, can be slaving away in the kitchen and look like that?" must be a common reaction to seeing the elegant Pascale wearing an uncreased and unspattered white shirt, hair neatly coiffed, holding up a delicious supper.'

Lorraine was the cover girl on the *Observer* magazine in April 2011, *Red Magazine* in December 2011 – 'Lorraine Pascale's totally lazy Christmas; it's stylish, simple and stress-free', on a special anniversary edition of *Good Housekeeping* in October 2012 – 'Lorraine Pascale on living the dream and staying slim on cake', and *The Sunday Times* magazine that same month – 'Look at these naughty girls getting flour all over their pretty Marni frocks! Model turned cook Lorraine Pascale was the focus of a kid-friendly baking feature. Lorraine and her mini kitchen assistants cooked up a storm, whilst fabulously attired in Roksanda Ilincic and Marni! Not many mothers would let their little ones near a sticky spatula in their very best dress but what a fabulously fun way to style a shoot!' Inside was a picture of Lorraine looking as pristine as ever in a purple dress and with her two little helpers under the headline 'Sticky Little Fingers'. The accompanying prose extolled the virtues of cooking alongside children: 'Dustings of flour and sticky handprints covering every surface; expectant faces gazing up at the kitchen worktop; a wooden spoon just crying out to be licked... Cooking alongside children is a messy, chaotic, but ultimately joyful experience, one we should cherish rather than fear. Baking is the best way to get kids involved in the kitchen, says Lorraine Pascale, the model turned cook who has taken the nation by storm with her relaxed, achievable approach to home cooking'.

Lorraine was also on the front cover of the October/November 2012 issue of the UK edition of *Marie Claire* magazine for a 'Black Beauty and Style in the British Media 2012' article, the *Daily Mail*'s *Weekend* magazine in November 2012 and *The Times* Saturday magazine that same month – 'Lorraine cuts a fine figure in this season's must-have items, tailored trousers and sharp jacket suits, to show you're really serious about celebrating this Christmas. Once you've got your wardrobe sorted, head to the kitchen to whip up one of Lorraine's devastatingly delicious and simple canapés, including a quick-cook canapé crostini, crunchy black pepper halloumi dipsticks with harissa houmous, sticky Asian BBQ chicken wings and bacon and mature Cheddar cheese twisties...' Readers were invited to go online and watch Lorraine 'strike her poses' as she modelled clothes from designers such as Ralph Lauren, Christian Louboutin and one of her favourites, All Saints. Or you could download an app, 'hover over the page and Lorraine will then begin to move before your very eyes'. She also made another appearance in *i-D* magazine in March 2009 as 'the former *i-D* cover star who renounced modelling to follow her one true passion in life – cake baking! Yum!' Accompanied by Jacob Sutton's pictures, the piece was good publicity for her newly found Bakehouse – 'Each cake is bespoke, the designs are modern, we only use the best ingredients and of course they are utterly delicious.'

Lorraine also caused something of a storm when a 1992 picture of her taken by photographer Bob Carlos Clarke – described as 'one of the great photographic image-makers of the last few decades' – went on show at the Little Black Gallery in Chelsea in April 2011. The black and white image featured her wearing a mass of plumes on her head and a bolero lamé top – and nothing else. The shot was taken from a side angle giving it some modesty, but gallery owner Ghislain Pascal said it had caused 'much amusement.' Other pictures on display by Clarke (who died in 2006) were more controversial. Indeed, the outside of the gallery was blacked out to create a peep show atmosphere. But it was said that his picture of Lorraine was one of the photographer's favourites from his 30-year career and he kept it on the wall of his studio for many years.

There was good news for those who felt Lorraine should never have given up modelling. Although she had already returned to the catwalk for the London Fashion Week show in New York in 2009, Lorraine only confirmed three years later that she might make it a regular thing, saying: 'I would like to model again. I'd be up for the catwalk too, as long as they would be happy to have a size 10–12 model.' She had certainly not been forgotten in some quarters. In an article hailing the success of black Montego Bay model Trissan Holder in November 2011, the *Kingston Gleaner* said that Holder's 'exotic and androgynous looks' had not only 'found favour with some of fashion's major players' but that she was being likened to Lorraine, whose 'memorable gap-tooth' made her a '*Vogue* favourite throughout the 80s.'

It remains to be seen whether Lorraine will ever grace the pages of *Vogue* or tread the catwalk again, although she will of course always be pictured in newspapers and magazines alongside features in which she talks about her charities and her cooking. Lorraine is keeping her options open. 'I don't love it in the same way I love cookery, but if it's a great publication and a great shoot, it's a fun thing to do.'

After deciding to make modelling a lesser part of her life, Lorraine spent the next few years trying a variety of often very unglamorous jobs in a bid to find out what career would really satisfy her. 'I wanted to do something different, so I made a list of everything I enjoyed, even if they seemed silly things, and tried to figure out a way to make them into a career.' And she already had experience of what she didn't want to do. As a teenager one of her first jobs was ironing neighbours' sheets at £1 an hour. Then she spent one Easter holiday on what she called 'turkey patrol' at Waitrose. Animal activists had been injecting the turkeys with substances and it was Lorraine's job to keep a watch on the birds. 'I had to make sure they were safe. I spent 39 hours a week standing there looking at frozen turkeys.' But now it was time for decisions to be made (at one time Lorraine had thought seriously about joining the police). She had not wasted the long hours at modelling assignments and spent the time reading and finding out what opportunities were around. It was a case of 'taking courses and experimenting, trying to find something I could do; towards a goal and something I could make a career out of.'

Self-confessed 'petrolhead' Lorraine (she would later book herself on a day learning to race at Silverstone) decided to expand her passion for racing cars with a practical training. Early in 2001 she undertook a mechanic's apprenticeship at the Skoda garage Adamsons in Deal, Kent. Such was the novelty of a statuesque black model hot from New York not only taking on a job on the outskirts of the seaside town,

Lorraine looking typically glamorous at the world premiere of *Gambit*, where she rubbed shoulders with the likes of Colin Firth and Cameron Diaz.

© Getty Images

Where it all began, a young Lorraine makes her mark in the fashion world after being scouted for her model potential at the tender age of 16.

Above: Aged 19, Lorraine struts her stuff across catwalks around the world.

Below: Amongst fashion royalty, Lorraine celebrates 25 years of London Fashion Week alongside the British Fashion Council in 2009.

© Rex Fea

sing alongside friend and fellow chef Gizzi Erskine at the launch of The French undry pop-up restaurant at Harrods, London.

Lorraine still knows how to work the camera at events across the country.

Above left: Showing off those pins on the red carpet.

Above right: Ambassador Lorraine attends a comedy gala in aid of the Prince's Trust.

Below left: Posing at a screening of *Silver Linings Playbook* hosted at the luxury Charlotte Street Hotel, London, 2012.

Below right: One step ahead at the VIP preview day for the Chelsea Flower Show, 2012

rraine with Sarah Brown and Trish Halpin at the *Marie Claire* Inspire and Mentor
rty in Leicester Square, London, 2011.

© *Getty Images*

With multiple television series a
best-selling books under her che
apron, Lorraine's cookery care
goes from strength to strength
she attends the Women in Film a
Television awards in 20

© Rex Feat

but one in a usually predominantly male field, that she caused a bit of a stir locally. Lorraine has said that her time tucked away in the garage workshop went unnoticed – but not so in the local press for she was visited by a photographer and reporter. She also featured in a news item for local news station Meridian. Newsman Iain McBride was despatched to cover the story in a follow up to a report by Meridian the night before about a chiropodist who was embarking on a new career as a male model. 'Tonight, we bring you the story of the supermodel who's forging a new career as a car mechanic' was how the news item was announced on 30 March.

For the eight or nine months she worked there, Lorraine would regularly travel down from London each weekend, don her overalls and get stuck in before returning home for the rest of the week. She was still modelling at this time and found that a permanent career lying under and leaning over cars was not for her, although she admits: 'I did have fun for a while and it did come in handy because now I can fix my own car.'

This was followed by a stint with 'super' hypnotist Paul McKenna, first learning some of his art and then enrolling on a course at the London College of Clinical Hypnosis (LCCH) after talking to a couple of friends who had done the same. She was then allowed to watch McKenna at work and progressed to being an assistant on his week-long 'Change Your Life in Seven Days' courses. The two are still Twitter friends. 'I found it all quite intriguing,' she has said. But there is no chance of getting to stare into Lorraine's eyes nowadays and hoping to change your life in seven days – or even less. For she has admitted that she has forgotten how to do it all.

During this job-seeking time Lorraine has confessed she tried 'a hundred different things', abandoning most courses halfway through. She was constantly 'dabbling'. This included training to be a secretary, a photographer and an interior designer, the latter she has described as 'fun – well, the shopping was, not so much the actual design'.

There could be a reason for Lorraine's dipping into so many career possibilities, apart from the fact she had simply not found her calling. She feels that having left home at 16 and being 'self-employed' since then made her realise she was better at working for herself. 'Working for other people... Oh, I'm not very good at being told what to do, let's put it like that. I think it is a case of if you have always been self-employed it's very difficult to be employed and vice-versa.'

With a young daughter to care for, Lorraine was also seeking a job that allowed her a more flexible lifestyle. She has since admitted that deciding to quit modelling and find a completely different career was certainly full of thwarted attempts and a lot of doubts.

'I was very nervous when I wanted to change, some people are supportive and some people aren't and there's often a nagging voice saying "Oh no, don't be stupid, you can't do that." That could have been a teacher at school or a parent, or just your own voice. So just make that voice your friend and do it anyway! It's okay to make mistakes and it's okay to fall down. Take your time and make small steps on the way to find what you really want to do.'

Lorraine, a fervent Manchester United supporter, even turned her hand to writing about the sport. The project was aimed at women and was described as the definitive guide to football especially for girls – 'a quick and easy reference book containing all the things you ever wanted to know about the game; the rules, the participants, the competitions, the business, everything in fact down to the song sheet'. Literary agent Darley Anderson promised it would 'do for football what David Essayon's *Expert* books did for gardening.' Published in 2005, the book was written while Lorraine was living in London. With a girly twist, the cover featured a football and a lipstick under the words 'Kick It'. Unfortunately, despite its blurb of 'OK girls, enough is enough. We've sat around for far too long on the sofa twiddling our thumbs watching our men get excited to a degree which rivals Saturday night in the bedroom. Football is threatening to take over our lives and our men unless we do something pretty damn quickly' and the assurance female footie fans would, for the first time in their lives be able to scream 'Oi ref! Offside!' the book, with Lorraine's name on the front, did not actually make the bookshops here in Britain, the home of football. It was published in Germany – 'snapped up in a spirited auction', allegedly – under the title *The Ultimate Football Book for Women* – or rather, *Das ültimative Fußballbuch für Frauen.*

Eventually after taking all those small steps and making some mistakes along the way Lorraine did find what she wanted to do. This came in 2005 when she enrolled at the prestigious Leiths School of Food and Wine in west London. The whole experience, she has said, 'captivated' her. There is some confusion over which course Lorraine took at the school. Some reports have her saying she enrolled on the evening class course – each six-week session currently costs £520 – and also that she was there on the three-term Diploma in Food and Wine aimed at 'those with professional chef ambitions' and designed 'for those who would like a career in food', which cost somewhat more – just under £7,000 at the time of writing. But it promised a 'comprehensive professional training that will ensure a rounded knowledge of food and a clear idea of current trends'.

The Diploma teaches fundamental cookery techniques – a very much back-to-basics curriculum – such as making batters, stocks, pastry and preparing meat and fish. But even on this course, the recipes of chicken sauté Normande and pork tenderloin with cherry tomato and pumpkin chutney seem challenging to the amateur cook! But for Lorraine, just finding something she immediately took to was an absolute joy despite the challenges. She said: 'I fell in love with it on the first day. I thought, "I've arrived". I imagined it would be women sitting around doing Victorian sponges. I didn't realise it was going to be tantrums, tiaras, arguments, people storming out, people quitting. It was tough. Hard.'

If there was a culinary 'Eureka!' moment for Lorraine, it came at one of the times when she was doing what she loves most – cooking – during the preparation of a fairly simple butternut squash soup but with her own twist on it with chilli and ginger – 'It just blew me away'. It was then, she says, that she knew she wanted to be a chef. She and the other students faced tests every week, an exam every month and then a final, hugely demanding test at the end. But Lorraine took it all in her stride. 'It was like putting on the right clothes or shoes or something. It just all fitted.'

She is now listed amongst the school's alumni, together with Tom Calver, who has appeared on TV with Jamie Oliver in Channel 4's *Jamie's Great Britain* (and who also featured in the accompanying book of the series), former BBC Good Food Award winner Gizzi Erskine, co-presenter of Channel 4's *Cook Yourself Thin* and *Cookery School*, and Matt Tebbutt, UKTV's *Market Kitchen* presenter.

Not everyone has been impressed with Lorraine's decision to attend Leiths, though. One internet critic commented: 'Could you afford £19,899 for 9 months with a £1,500 deposit straight up? Would you do that for your girl!? Because your girl can cook well!? That is the kind of money you are looking at if you thought you could get a degree from Leiths School of food, wine and promises, which is one of Lorraine's prides. There are not a lot of people who can reject working in a professional kitchen and then are able to set up their own business. Could you?'

But Lorraine had found the passion she had been searching for and she later broke into her money reserve to take a two-year foundation degree in International Culinary Arts in Pastry at Thames Valley University costing just under £20,000. Described as a highly specialised course for 'practising pastry working in the hospitality industry', it is aimed at leading students to senior positions as chefs. The course was intense and covered all aspects of pastry making as well as kitchen management. Tutorials included demonstrations and practical cooking lessons, as well as menu planning, budgeting and wine appreciation. Official 'tester' for her resulting dishes was daughter Ella – 'She'd come home and there would be like, four pies and six pizzas on the table to try!'

Like her fellow students, Lorraine also had to prepare a working document to show future employers. The degree course gives the option to go on to the final year of a BA (Hons) in International Culinary Arts, which includes international gastronomy, food policy and micro-biology. Incredibly, despite her already hectic workload and commitments, Lorraine decided to embark on the course. Like the other students, she had to write a 10,000-word dissertation and her assessments were made on 'assignments, examinations, portfolios or work, group work, presentations, reports and self-reflection'. Despite breaks from the course because of work commitments she eventually passed with First Class Honours in 2012.

Always conscious of her interrupted education when young, Lorraine has an almost burning desire to keep learning now. She says it keeps her grounded in the hectic world of TV stardom; keeps her 'sane'.

And so Lorraine had at last found her dream job – one that might have been 'quirky' and 'odd' (her words) compared to previous career choices but, using the word she often uses now to describe doing what she loves, it provoked a 'passion' in her. Although comment about the high cost of the Leiths' course may be valid, the reference to dismissing practical experience in professional kitchens is not. For Lorraine did just that. She spent just under a year perfecting her art with stints in several kitchens including the two-Michelin-star The Square restaurant and Hakkasan in Mayfair, Petrus (one of fiery chef Gordon Ramsay's eateries) and The Mandarin Oriental, both in Knightsbridge, The Wolseley in Piccadilly and Tom Aikens Restaurant with its Michelin à la carte menu in Chelsea – a lot of restaurants in what Lorraine has described as a 'very brief spell' – with even briefer spells (around a month or less) spent at each one.

But Lorraine faced the dilemma many working mothers have – the time spent away from her child. She was unhappy that the unsociable hours did not fit easily with being a single parent and were not allowing her enough time with daughter Ella. Often she would be working an 18-hour day, leaving home at 6am and not getting away until midnight.'It really wasn't working out for me and it was hard to live a life.' It wasn't so much the hard graft and long working hours that made Lorraine come to her decision to quit – she has always been an early riser and is never afraid of putting her back into work – there was another, more poignant reason. With her background and all the accompanying childhood anxieties, Lorraine had one major fear: that her tough schedule would have drastic results. 'I realised I wouldn't be around very long with the pace I was setting,' she has admitted. And she had always to be there for her daughter – 'to sleep and spend time with Ella'.

So Lorraine switched tack and began working days at a branch of the Hummingbird Bakery – specialists in American cupcakes, brownies, pies and desserts. She got her job there by answering an advertisement on the Catering Vacancies section of the gumtree.com website. After nine months at Hummingbird Lorraine had the incentive to start her own cake business. Initially she went 'gluten-free' – 'Because every woman thinks they've got a problem with wheat. Only of course – we haven't.' This was a personal view from Lorraine because around then medical problems led doctors to diagnose her as suffering from coeliac disease (having intolerance to wheat, barley and rye). Luckily, for someone who was to make their future living out of cooking – including baking her own special bread – it turned out not to be the case. But the suggestion was enough to prompt her early attempt to set up a gluten-free cake-making company, although it was not as successful as she had hoped.

Lorraine started Glutilicious Ltd in January 2007 with the aim of catering exclusively for the gluten-free diners of the world, but the company ceased trading 18 months later. It was back to basics with her home baking, and deciding that her cupcakes and desserts should simply taste delicious – although Lorraine still ensures some of her wares are indeed gluten-free.

Lorraine worked flat out in her little kitchen at home in west London, doing everything from ordering ingredients to baking, taking orders and generally managing the business. She then hired staff and production of the cakes moved to Battersea. Gritting her teeth she would often brave the cold to set up a stall at a market in Clapham from which she sold her cakes. Being self-employed obviously brought new problems. For a start there was no regular income and so the pressure was on – 'I was used to knowing where the next pay cheque was coming from and that kind of thing.' But Lorraine was determined to make it work.

It was her friend Marco Pierre White who suggested she should approach Selfridges. The store's food director at the time was Ewan Venters, who saw something special in Lorraine. He commissioned 200 handmade Christmas/party cakes from her in 2008. The store kindly let Lorraine use its kitchen 'in the bowels of the building' to meet the order, working from 7am until 11pm each day. It took her 19 days to complete the order. (Later she became so busy that she ended up renting a large kitchen.) Seeing all the cakes lined up on the shelves was, according to Lorraine, 'an amazing feeling'.

Her efforts did not go unnoticed by the glossy

magazines she had once graced as a model. Indeed she whizzed around London on her red Vespa, buttering up the press. On 28 November 2008 *Vogue* reported: 'While she might have spent most of the Nineties as one of the most successful fashion models in the world (working alongside Kate Moss, Naomi Campbell and Christy Turlington), the only thing occupying the mind of Lorraine Pascale of late is cooking. And now the former face of Versace and Donna Karan is the official Celebration Cake Supplier for Selfridges department store for the festive season. Dubbed the next Jane Asher of the cake world by Selfridges' food director Ewan Venters, Pascale (who enrolled on a fulltime Diploma of Food and Wine course at Leiths, the renowned cookery school, and has worked in the kitchens of The Wolseley and The Mandarin Oriental to name but just a few), has created a rich rum flavoured cake. Handcrafted and enveloped in thick white icing, the cake is packed full of vine fruits, cherries and citrus peel with a delicate hint of spice. Pascale will also be creating bespoke celebration cakes for the department store. The Lorraine Pascale Christmas cake costs £29.99 and is available now from Selfridges.' Another reviewer purred: 'She only takes commissions but her cakes are unbelievably delicious and her decorations are much more exciting than the run-of-the-mill rosebuds and butterflies. She recently did the cakes for the launch of cult eyewear brand, Prism London, and coordinated the icing with the colours in the Prism range.'

Lorraine's research on setting up a business meant she knew you have to get out there and let people know what you have on offer. So she cleverly wooed contacts and the media, calling in on style-leading magazines such as *Grazia*, which reported: '"I'd always wanted to do something more creative when I was modelling," she told us when she dropped by Grazia's offices today with a box of cupcakes which were promptly devoured. "I wanted my cakes to be lighter and fluffier than anything else out there, and I didn't want them to look twee so mine are raunchy and sexy." How can a cupcake be sexy? I hear you think. They are decorated with red icing stilettoes for a start. But you've got to eat one to experience what she means. Her naughty little cupcakes are sold in Selfridges, and she is, she tells us, "working on fondant fancies, to move it on from the cupcake." Naughty but nice.' In a further promotion for the Bakehouse, Lorraine gave a rundown of her average day – or as it was called 'A Day in Lorraine's World':

'I wake up at 5.30am each morning. I don't need much sleep. The sun streams through my bedroom window, one eye opens and then the mind starts ticking. I try to meditate for ten minutes to get some focus, and then starting making my 12-year-old daughter Ella, breakfast. I take her to school and then (if I'm feeling good) I'll spend half an hour in the gym before hurrying home to check my emails for orders, and then have a shower. 9.30am: I eat breakfast as I'm dashing out the door, and it's usually toasted rye bread – yummy! After this I jump on my trusty Vespa and it's off to meetings.'

You can understand, having worked her way through the traditional and challenging route of learning how to cook, why Lorraine gets frustrated when her ability is doubted. Her determination sometimes means neglecting the family she loves, though. When writing her books, for instance, she gets so engrossed that she does not stay as involved with them as she would like to. 'I do often feel lots of guilt for not spending time with them when I am hard at work,' she has admitted. So, like thousands of other working mothers, Lorraine is often torn between her family and her career. It's a difficult juggling act. And it isn't as if success came overnight. She didn't just spring up as TV's Smiley Chef, she underwent five years' training and worked extremely hard to get there. Even today, with fame and success she can get by on four hours' sleep a night, ever-anxious to simply be up and doing – or be awake until the early hours (4am is her record!) working out new recipes on her laptop. She keeps a notebook with her at all times to jot down recipe ideas and a 'to do' list.

In all, Lorraine spent a good few years mastering her

art. She is now happy to have proved the cynicism she initially faced was completely misplaced. 'Friends readied themselves to tease me yet again about another failed venture but this time I surprised them all. I just kept on going with the course and I ended up studying cookery, specialising in patisserie, for over a decade. I cut my teeth working in some of the country's most respected kitchens, and I worked alongside chefs who were completely committed to pursuit of culinary perfection.' You can understand why she hates the cynical view that she is just a leggy clothes horse who happened to get lucky. 'There was a lot of negativity and jokes from others when I was doing all these courses. A lot of people were laughing at me and saying, "What's she doing, why doesn't she just stick to modelling?" It was quite hard but I kept going.'

It was Lorraine's mother who gave her great support during this time. Lorraine uses the word 'grafter' a lot when talking about working hard at whatever project she has set her mind to. It was her mum who said that failure only comes when you stop trying – 'So I kept trying!' And in all aspects of her life but with particular reference to her sad marriage, Lorraine says: 'I've followed up on my mother's principles of being honest and it's going well.' And although she says that her adoptive parents gave her 'great guidance' in other areas, 'as far as inner strength goes, I think it must be from nature.'

Chapter 6

Cupcake Queen

After signing the lease in June 2009, Lorraine opened her first retail operation, Ella's Bakehouse, in London's Covent Garden, installing ovens and using other kitchen equipment she had bought second hand on eBay. 'With a client list that includes Guy Ritchie and Marco Pierre White, Ella's Bakehouse is tipped for big things. You'll find quality baked goods, including legendary cupcakes, as well as a range of specialist coffees and teas set in a diner style café with plenty of seating,' was how the Covent Garden London website described it.

But her plans to name the shop after her daughter and, indeed, to one day open a chain of stores under the same name, were later thwarted by a legal wrangle. She had to change the name to 'Cupcake Bakehouse' in June 2012 after another company, Ella's Kitchen, complained the two names were too similar. (The founder of Ella's Kitchen, Paul Lindley, also named his business after his daughter, Ella.) The Intellectual Property Office, which handles applications to register names, also ordered Lorraine to pay £2,000 costs. Today, business is booming at Lorraine's little Covent Garden cupcake specialist shop which as well as being somewhere to pop into for coffee and cake, also makes up orders for individual requests. 'If you want to personalise your cakes and cupcakes, all you need do is contact the lovely people in store and they can whip up a personalised piece of perfection in no time...'

Lorraine puts as much effort into the shop as she does everything else in her life, reading relevant business books, scouring websites and gleaning as much information as she could from a friend. But the relentless hard work at getting the business off the ground, with mishaps and disappointments, nearly broke her. 'I suppose I did not realise that it would be so hard setting up my own business. There became no such thing as "after work" or "weekends" as I was working all the time. Mistakes I made were not asking for help when I felt like I was sinking!'

Lorraine is often buoyed up at difficult times by

reflecting on uplifting quotes from the famous (she is a great reader), which she says inspire her to carry on. In this case, she said it was the great Winston Churchill's belief that 'When you're going through hell, keep going' which made her persevere. And the Bakehouse was certainly winning fans. In May 2009 the *Observer*'s Polly Vernon described Lorraine as 'the world's least likely cake-maker. She's 36 years old and beautiful: leggy, sleek, ineffably glam, the kind of slender that suggests daily exercise and minimal exposure to candy-coloured confection.' The article was accompanied by three pictures by Suki Dhanda of Lorraine wearing chef's whites and a head-gripping black scarf, while wielding a whisk and a bowl. Then in June 2009 London's *Metro* wrote enthusiastically about Lorraine and her new breed of exotic and colourful cupcakes under the headline 'She's Cool for Cakes': 'Excuse the sweeping statement but bakers tend to be rotund chaps with exceedingly soft hands. Today, however, it's hard not to keep ogling moronically. As well as glittery cupcakes and florid wedding cakes, there are "couture cakes" with red lips and stiletto toppings. Amidst all this is baker Lorraine Pascale, the former face of Versace, Bambi-limbed and radiant, oblivious to cream stuck in her fringe like a naughty toddler. How refreshing... Indeed, she's rocking the fusty cake world. Think French baking with a new eccentric, Anglo twist.'

Lorraine herself spoke about some of her more experimental cupcake creations: 'I made some small cakes with white icing, black heels and black lips for a fashion party. At home I've been trying bra and underwear-set couture cakes. I did a cocktail glass but it didn't work... This guy wanted his wife's chest so I had a picture of it as I worked. They'd be good for Valentine's Day – boobs and bums. Although I went to Bruges and saw a shop doing chocolate willies – I'm not doing that!' She had also made T-shirt, Stud Muffin and Real Men Eat cakes ('because we need to get the men eating cake'.) The article finished just as breathlessly. 'Eyes alight, she adds with pride: "Most bakers don't use vanilla pods, they use essence. I scrape the vanilla pods out and put the seeds in the sugar syrup for extra flavour. I also put seeds in my vanilla cream toppings." For a finale, the white chocolate cheesecake comes out before she stuffs ten cupcakes in my cycle pannier and she's back to the stove.'

Others picked up on the whole new cupcake phenomenon, one which now saw the little sugary wares as more than just baking. 'In a time where all cupcakes are not to be treated as equals, Lorraine's cupcakes definitely reign supreme. Whether it's her American-inspired flavours, French-inspired sponges, or glitter-dusted frosting, there is definitely something special about Ella's Bakehouse. And I think that special something might just be a Ms Lorraine Pascale,' reported Cate Sevilla on website bitchbuzz in February 2010.

Early public reviews of the Cupcake Bakehouse (when it was still Ella's) were mixed, especially from foreign visitors:

'It's a small and cute cupcake shop with a few seats. So we tried lemon curd and carrot cupcakes. We drunk hot Earl Grey tea and as we expected, the cupcakes were tasty because they should be homemade. Just the topping was a little bit very sweet.'

'Classy cupcakes and pleasing presentation. Though I have eaten better ones and the place is on the small side, it is full of charm.'

'Keep in mind, I write this as an American, for what it's worth. It may be cupcakes in London are a different animal, and Ella's cupcakes really are fantastic to someone with a European palate ... but I doubt it highly. When I first saw Ella's, I thought it was a sanctuary on a cold, rainy morning. The service was quick and attentive, the shop was clean, the options plentiful. But the cupcakes? Awful. The cake itself was dry and reminiscent of a stale muffin left in the refrigerator too long. The frosting tasted like cheap margarine. It was not fluffy or light, but sat like a dense pat of lard on my poor excuse for a cake. I took two bites, and discretely threw the rest in the trash. I will not be returning.'

British cupcake quaffers seemed happier:

'The cupcakes themselves should get five stars, but because it's so small and fills up quite quickly, I usually have to sit outside. (COLD and cupcakes don't mix!) The staff are always friendly, the cupcakes always delicious, and the tea is always strong. Basically, it's fantastic! (Just don't count on getting a seat!)'

'The peanut butter frosting with edible glitter alone is worth travelling miles for. A regular builder's tea and a cupcake comes to just £2.80, which has got to be a bargain in expensive Covent Garden. Cupcake was soft, moist, nutty with loads of peanut butter frosting.'

'I was going to go for the usual red velvet cupcake – who doesn't love red velvet? – but there was a lone coffee cupcake calling my name. It surely did not disappoint.'

That same year, Lorraine cocked a snook at not always going for the, shall we say, low-calorie approach to cooking. She teamed up with Mars Maltesers in a competition to 'inspire amateur cooks to unleash their inner domestic goddess'. The only rule of the challenge was, of course, that the recipes should feature Maltesers – 'the much-loved ingredient'. The winner would get to sell their Malteser marvel at Lorraine's Bakehouse (then still called Ella's) as well as receiving a food processor and a supply of Maltesers 'to inspire them to create more chocolatey masterpieces'.

Warming to her theme, Lorraine said: 'I've always been a fan of Maltesers and they're a fantastic addition to sweet treats. The recipe sold in Ella's Bakehouse will be highly creative, look fantastic and most importantly, be fun to make and eat.' Lorraine's own 'sinfully delightful' Maltesers cake – which did exactly what it said on the tin – was literally piles of the chocolates on a sponge cake covering it completely. She called it 'Let them Eat Cake, Cake'. The cake came about when Lorraine and Ella were experimenting in the kitchen, and was originally covered with M&Ms (they won't like this but Lorraine said that though it 'looked very cool, it just wasn't me so we came up with a worthy substitute' – at least both are made by the same company, Mars).

One reviewer commented: 'There comes a time in your life when you just have to go for it, and try to make the richest, sweetest, chocolateyest (is that a word? Definitely should be!) cake possible.'

There were also the Maltesers cheesecake ('wickedly crunchy') and the chocolate fridge cake (containing crushed Maltesers) and of course Maltesers cupcakes – 'an irresistible combination of cake, buttercream and crunchy bits of Maltesers. You'll definitely need to hide these from the kids!' – so Lorraine really had put her mouth where the chocolate is in respect of the brand. Incidentally, the winning entry in the competition was a Maltesers chocolate layered cake.

And not one to miss an opportunity, Lorraine opened up a 'pop-up' Ella's Bakehouse store during London Fashion Week in 2010. Said one couture/culinary commentator: 'Even with all the fashion madness going on, we still need sugary treats to keep us going. I reckon even weary and famished fashion editors won't be able to resist a "couture cupcake" from pop-up store, Ella's Bakehouse.' Word was certainly going round. Lorraine was interviewed for a *Daily Mail* article 'Ladies Who Launch' in February 2010 in a list of 'female entrepreneurs who don't let the recession get in the way of their dreams'. Gushed Lorraine: 'Our lemon-raspberry is the most popular. People fall in love with our cakes instantly. I think people indulge in smaller things in tough times, which is why lipstick is selling so well right now, too. I work long hours, but gone are the days when I would bake nonstop for 19 hours – I now employ a small team of people [she has a team of 10 nowadays] and spend a lot of my time in meetings. At the moment I'm looking at new sites for more Ella's Bakehouses. There are still teething problems. People say, "You have to hang in there for the first year as it is a little tough…" Well, it's a lot tough!' She admitted that she 'barely' slept, that the hours 'can seem endless' and her jeans sometimes felt as if they had shrunk in the wash because of all the tasting she had to do.

Lorraine made the move from being behind the scenes to in front of the cameras following the suggestion of a friend who thought Lorraine's experience of being photographed might bode well for TV. Getting someone to take on a complete newcomer was not easy even though she was being recognised on the London circuit and invited to events in her capacity as a chef – including attending the opening of the revamped River Terrace Café with Sarah Doukas in May 2010. However, Lorraine was turned down by a few TV agents before finding one who would take her on. 'We knocked on lots of doors to get noticed,' she said.

In 2010, Lorraine found herself an agent (she is now signed up with James Grant Media Management), had endless meetings and filmed a pilot cookery programme, which was taken up by the BBC. The rest, as they say, is history.

Chapter 7

Success – and staying slim

One of the regular questions Lorraine gets asked is how she manages to stay so slim when most of her time is spent cooking – and sampling – her calorie-laden dishes. (As the *Daily Mirror* once commented: 'She comes in for a bit of stick, but Lorraine Pascale comes over as a really bubbly presence. Doesn't really look as if she's ever tasted a chip in anger, mind...') The answer is she doesn't – not when recipe creation is taking place anyway. Lorraine can put on a stone in weight during those recipe-testing sessions – times when she will 'eat, eat, eat'. So she certainly isn't about to eat everything she prepares for the cameras too – 'Of course I don't eat every single thing I cook on the shows. I cook seven dishes for four to six people for each episode.'

There is also her love of pasta (brown, not white), potatoes, cakes and bread – and the occasional takeaway. But she has said that most of the time her everyday diet is nothing like she presents on her shows. 'I eat a balanced diet and cakes are for treats. I eat lots of veggies and a good amount of meat and fish. If I have a heavy carb day, the next will be much more protein-based. But it's nonsense to say I don't eat my own food – I'm a chef.'

But Lorraine spends a lot more time keeping in shape than she lets on. She works out and exercises – including boxing and lots of heavy weight-training around four times a week – to keep the pounds off. At the gym her workout includes overhead bar work to tone her arms. At home she takes to the treadmill running up a sweat to her favourite 80s and 90s music from Spandau Ballet, Level 42 and The Eurythmics (her favourite song from the latter is 'There Must be an Angel'). She also runs. 'I'm like any other woman. When I run round the park – which is not nearly often enough – I hate every second.'

Her disciplined routine shows, that despite her protestations, looking good takes time and effort. But she was certainly no different from any other woman when she was pregnant with Ella. It is hard to believe looking at her now, but Lorraine piled on four-and-a-half stone after giving in to the temptation of cravings – especially baby new potatoes soaked in 'about half a ton of Flora'. Back then the otherwise slimline Lorraine actually had a stomach. She also, she has confessed, had a bottom that stuck out!

Unlike most weight-conscious women Lorraine says she does not weigh herself regularly – jumping on the scales only once a year at her annual medical check-up. And even then, she has said she declines to know what the scales say. This may not be strictly true for she has admitted to nowadays weighing 68 kilos (10st 9lb) compared to the 58 kilos (9st 1lb) of her modelling days. But it is heartening to know that she has good days and bad days and loves her food. 'One day I could make baked fish, and the next day it's a full-on baked Camembert with garlic and a massive ham with all the trimmings!' And just in case you think Lorraine concentrates only on calorie-laden food for her TV-viewing public, she has actually created a low-fat Skinny Little Tart made with filo pastry, light yoghurt and fruit!

One still wonders how she keeps that figure with her love of Chorizo (Spanish spicy sausage), which she puts in 'everything' including omelettes, bread and casseroles as well as eating it 'neat' from the fridge. Then there is her fondness for prawn-cocktail-flavoured crisps, Frazzles and Hula Hoops. In fact, Lorraine has said that she can't recall a day when she hasn't munched away on a packet of crisps! And after a long day in the kitchen she is more than ready to order a takeaway. She insists she doesn't care if she is a size 10 or 14, so long as her trousers look good on her, and that she sets a good eating example to her teenage daughter. But undoubtedly Lorraine's strict adherence to running and working out is what helps keep her in shape. And also, in short, she gets miffed about the continuous questioning and debate over the weight of television chefs such as herself and Nigella Lawson. 'Why is there such an obsession with how big Nigella is or how small she is – or how big or small I am? No one ever says anything about Gordon Ramsay's size – and he's pretty slim – or Gary Rhodes. It's ridiculous. I guess female chefs aren't allowed to be slim.'

Once you reach the top in the popularity and achievement stakes, you also start receiving invitations to events confirming your place in the rather elite band of the famous that have strived and succeeded (a completely different group to those who somehow become famous for being, well famous). And so it was in May 2011 Lorraine joined other successful women at London's W Hotel for the launch of *Marie Claire* magazine's Inspire & Mentor campaign. In association with The Prince's Trust, the campaign aimed to offer the magazine's readers the chance to be mentored by 25 of the most influential women in Britain (amongst those present were former PM's wife Sarah Brown).

Lorraine said she was there because she had enjoyed the support of people who had really helped her and now she wanted to do something for others. Among those who personally inspired her, she said, were the likes of Oprah Winfrey (Lorraine would love to have dinner and a chat with the mega successful American chat-show host, describing her as a 'tour de force'), whose optimism had touched her. (Showing that she does not just get involved with mainstream events, Lorraine had, the month before, led a panel of judges to find the winner of the London Pride cake, organised by the gay organisation Pride London.) Lorraine has also appeared as a guest on Channel 4's satirical quiz show *8 Out of 10 Cats* and on the ITV lunchtime programme, *Loose Women*.

In 2012 Lorraine continued her support for getting the most from a working life on a more basic level when she was at Westfield London Shopping Centre, in London's Shepherds Bush, with Skills Minister John Hayes to launch a new careers advisory service. She spoke about her own varied work history and promoted the National Careers Service by saying: 'Having independent careers advice can really help you find the thing you want to do. I'd encourage everyone to make the most of the National Careers Service to find out how to take their career forward, and realise their ambitions.'

So, did Lorraine make the right choice to abandon a

successful career as a model and turn her hand to cooking? The answer can only be a resounding 'yes'. Her books, which have sold over 540,000 in 20 months, have been bought eagerly as far afield as South Africa and Australia and outsold those of other TV chefs, only narrowly being beaten at one point by Jamie Oliver. Her TV programmes have been sold to over 60 countries. And despite her critics she has made an incredible success of what she does. In November 2011 she was pronounced one of London's 1,000 Most Influential People and in February 2012 it was announced that Lorraine was on the TV Rich list of celebrity magazine *OK!* as being one of the top ten highest-paid TV personalities, earning around £2m the previous year from all her business and television-linked projects. She was seventh on the list and only one of two women who were classified as having made it big financially – the other, incidentally, was former *The Only Way Is Essex* 'star' Amy Childs, who was placed equal second with TV funny man Harry Hill with her estimated earnings of £2.75m.

Lorraine also made it onto the International Women's Day Famous Female Cooks list the next month (together with the likes of older favourites such as Elizabeth David and Fanny Cradock and a more contemporary Delia Smith). Special praise went to her Mojito Genoese cake, toad in the hole and whoopie cakes.

Chapter 8

'Beautiful baker girl'

The main problem about being in the public eye, of course, is the public. The people who help nurture your fame and success can also be the ones who turn against you. And exposing yourself on television with skills as vulnerable and as subjective as cooking provokes passionate outpourings. And so it was on 10 January 2011 when Lorraine's first BBC cookery show, *Baking Made Easy*, appeared on television. Publicity material described her as 'chef, baker and patissier' with this first show kicking off 'with a feat of baking engineering – Parmesan and poppy seed lollipops'. There was also the making of soda bread, blueberry and lemon millefeuilles and the 'I Can't

Believe You Made That' cake – 'dramatic delicious and versatile'.

Lorraine had made an earlier cookery TV appearance, though, when she appeared on *Saturday Kitchen* presented by James Martin on New Year's Eve morning. She was introduced as 'a new face' and there were 'oohs' and 'aahs' after Martin said she would 'show us her macaroons'. Wearing her trademark white shirt Lorraine did just that, having first visited France to see how the French made them. The clip would later appear in her own series.

Lorraine's personal brief to her crew was to forget about what she looked like (no easy matter when she is so easy on the eye) but to make the food look 'positively pornographic'. This approach seemed to please TV viewers, with one commenting: 'She's gorgeous of course, but unlike dear Nigella, not overtly having sex with the camera!' Lorraine was to get bolder and a little more risqué two years later when the names she gave some of her dishes – such as 'Naughty Naughty Nachos' and 'Skinny Dipping' – gave rise to a competition for her fans to come up with their own cheeky recipe titles on her favourite social forum Twitter, #LorrainesFlirtyFood. The come-on was the invitation to think of 'tantalising titles' and 'sexy supper' names of your own. In return the winner would receive a signed copy of one of Lorraine's books.

Lorraine's first cookery series – with each episode taking a week to record – was said to centre on her 'passion for baking' and featured 'both sweet and savoury classics'. Indeed, her opening line was: 'Hello, I'm Lorraine Pascale and I'm passionate about baking...' Wearing a striped apron and holding a white mug, she had the responsibility of endearing herself to the ever-critical viewing public and proving herself as a television newcomer in a field that is so highly competitive.

It was certainly something of a learning curve for Lorraine. She had spent many years standing silently in front of a camera as a model, but she had never really talked to one for any length of time, especially with the added complications of commentating as she cooked, let alone in such a make or break debut. It was no wonder that she barely slept the night before recording because of nerves. When the big day came such was her exuberance that she found herself almost shouting her recipes until she was told to take it down a notch or two. 'It was as if I was doing a demonstration at school. The crew had to say, "You do have a microphone on, you don't have to shout." It took me a while to get into the groove.'

None of those nerves were obvious in her first broadcast, but regular viewers would have noted how her confidence in front of the camera grew, both in her 'studio kitchen' and as she whisked around London and other locations looking at ingredients as the series progressed. This may have been helped by the purchase of books on public speaking to give herself confidence. But rather than celebrate her first broadcast, an ever self-critical and unconfident Lorraine was at home hiding under the duvet. 'Everybody was asking me if I was having a party. No way!' This first series was also something of a challenge with its demand for new recipes and ideas and it was no wonder Lorraine had sleepless nights in the run-up to it. 'It's been very difficult. I've had to be really, really organised. I only sleep for five or six hours a night so you can kind of fit everything in.'

Each one of the six programmes provoked a reaction. There was the debut 'So Easy' then 'Speed Baking' ('two super-fast canapés, totally lazy mini sausage rolls and sun-dried tomato and rosemary palmiers. Both are made with shop-bought puff pastry with absolutely no guilt') in which Lorraine was also seen in Paris 'for inspiration', 'Modern Classics' ('Lorraine has an easy recipe for perfect meringue every time and it forms the base for an old-school pavlova. But there's a twist – spiced blackberry, pear and apple pavlova is Lorraine's modern take on that all-time favourite dessert'), 'Very Entertaining' ('Want stress-free ideas for entertaining? How about Lorraine Pascale's whisky and chilli tiger prawns?') 'Bake to Impress' ('If you want to impress with baking,

Lorraine Pascale has got it covered') and 'Time to Bake' ('Lorraine Pascale takes us through recipes to relax over, including pumpkin and rosemary muffins, which are good for breakfast, lunch or any time at all').

For Lorraine, that first series meant a single goal. '*Baking Made Easy* will raise my profile but the main thing is it will enable me to continue doing what I love – being in the kitchen, working with cookery books and making great food.'

The series, broadcast from a rented kitchen in Sheen, southwest London, because Lorraine's own kitchen was too small to accommodate a TV crew, had people flocking to the internet's open forum site – today's equivalent, some might say, of the thumb up or thumb down in a gladiator ring – to comment on TV's latest celebrity chef (and only one of two black ones to find fame on British TV). Lorraine's celebration/wedding red velvet cake, shown in the 7 February episode, was the main focus of public opinion:

'Good luck to her, but it's not for me. Red velvet cake – no, it was a red-coloured sponge. There's nothing new in terms of her cookery. It would be nice to have a programme that has a bit of innovation for a change. As for her cupcakes... I made the trip to her shop before the programme started and was very disappointed (inedible). I wrote to her regarding this and got no response.

Given her approach and profile, I was surprised not to get some kind of response. I'm sure she will continue to gain popularity but not as a result of skill and talent.'

'OMG. I'm sorry but as a professional cake decorator, including wedding cakes, I was shocked and appalled to see how she decorated the three-tier wedding cake. My brides would expect more than just "sticking on a dot to cover a mistake". The finish of the sugar paste was terrible. A good cake maker will take lots of time and care over a wedding cake. They are not knocked up in a couple of hours.'

'That three-tier cake was most certainly not breathtaking. Sorry, but an entire bottle of food colouring emptied into a cake, a different cake than the one that came out of the oven and not even levelled... I suggest you Google for cake makers and see how it's really done. Having said that, her other dishes looked nice.'

Writing for the *Mail* online on 6 February, Suzanne Moore did not seem sure whether she liked Lorraine – or her cooking – or not.

'Watching Lorraine Pascale making some focaccia

on telly the other night was a blessed relief. The ex-model is quite gorgeous, of course, but what I liked was her calmness and the fact that this was something I might possibly make.

'She wasn't shouting at me about her testicles. Or telling me the planet would end if I don't eat fish, or insisting I rear and kill my own pigs.

'Pascale is a sure sign that the cult of the celebrity chef is so tired that they couldn't even get a soufflé to rise if its main ingredient was Viagra. The superchefs seem to be imploding, flogging themselves to supermarkets after having told us supermarkets are evil. Like rock stars who are no longer hip, they have to find political causes to give them a purpose in life.'

Fortunately, there were definite Lorraine devotees too:

'I think she is brilliant. I could watch this programme all day long. Bash her all you like. She's successful, easy on the eye and I love her simple cookery methods.'

'Congratulations, Lorraine. You are a star in my book. This young woman is down to earth and explains cooking in a very simple language.'

The *Daily Mail*'s Nick McGrath seemed very smitten: 'Lorraine's infectious blend of culinary presentation is an appetising mixture of gastronomic onomatopoeia. I love the sound of words like, "dollop", "squidge", and "plop" – transparent enthusiasm for food and stunning looks and a show-stopping smile.'

So too was another male fan on the 'Sober in the Cauldron' website: 'Lorraine is beautiful and so sexy on her Vespa! I love watching her riding it. I think she's a natural on camera and really likeable. Her enthusiasm and positive attitude radiates through. And that smile, Jesus. Also, how great is it to see a gorgeous black woman presenting a food show. I just hope people give the show a chance. I'm sure men up and down the country will be tuning in!'

Although aimed at tying in with the BBC series the accompanying *Baking Made Easy* book was published on 6 January, four days before Lorraine first hit our television screens. In retrospect this was a pretty brave move for its success depended on whether or not the television-viewing public took to the newcomer. But it paid off. As one erudite critic, Sam Shetabi, commented: 'Lorraine burst on to the scene in 2011 and became a hugely successful new face for BBC Two. Her first series *Baking Made Easy* stays in my mind because of how it introduced an entirely new chef – a new 'character' if you will – to an unfamiliar audience. Over the six parts, you are introduced to, taught by and invited to suss out a whole new chef and their food. It's like character development in a drama, but with recipes, anecdotes and an inviting presentational style to give us our arc. Building this slow-burning introduction in to new series allows new cooking talent to connect to viewers. And become stars in their own right.'

In a canny marketing move, Lorraine's accompanying *Baking Made Easy* book was regularly caught on camera during the TV series. 'You would think being a top model, the first black British model to become the cover of American *Elle*, joining Kate Moss, Naomi Campbell, Elle Macpherson among others in Milan, Paris, and Rome would be a dream life. Not so, tired of prancing around in front of a camera modelling and not being allowed to speak, Lorraine wanted a new career – as a chef,' was the publicity blurb from her publisher HarperCollins, who hailed her as the new 'home baking heroine'.

The book, with warm acknowledgements from Lorraine to her family and friends – including mother Audrey, father Roger, brother Jason, stepmother Kate, half-sister Francesca and even her aunty Angela – contained 100 recipes – or '100 mouth-watering recipes for every kind of baked goody' as HarperCollins put it, adding: 'Urban, sexy, independent and effortlessly stylish Lorraine will be a breath of fresh air to the world of cookery'. However, no matter how much work and thought a chef puts into their book, there will always be those who find something to complain about. Most of the less positive reviews from readers were to say that the book did not contain enough photographs of the finished dishes – and that there were too many pictures of the model cook:

'I didn't exactly warm to Lorraine on the television but thought that I'd enjoy the book, which I do, but it has 26 photos of herself in the book! And not that many photos of the food! I don't get food writers who do that. I thought Sophie Dahl's book was bad and Rachel Allen is a serial offender but this was the worst for it!'

'Firstly like all the others before me said, there just aren't enough pictures. I've tried three of the recipes and they just did not work. Not going to try another recipe, instead going to see if I can sell it on eBay, and see if I can get at least some of the money back that I spent on this book.'

'I do like to have a picture to show what it is I'm preparing, how it should look etc, and there are quite a few that have no pictures and are the recipes alone.'

There was the occasional anti Lorraine remark, too:

'I found this book a fairly typical BBC "let's capitalise on the series", and produced in a hurry. The print quality and the colour photography were poorer than the original price warranted and there were only a few pictures of the actual cakes. Also, LP had an overtly wide definition of baking so anything that goes into an oven qualifies as baking according to her definition. The breads, cakes and pies were nothing special and, in the case of one loaf, downright dreadful. Her macaroons recipe is distinctly odd, requiring them to be piped onto the baking sheet to make the standard round macaroon. I'm glad I got this book very cheap so I won't feel so bad about having taken it to the charity shop. She is a personable presenter for a TV programme but, gals, never trust a thin baker…'

'I would now NOT recommend this book. I know that many reviews here fully support the book, and their only quibble is over the lack of photos for each recipe (yes, I agree with that too). But three out of three recipes have failed for me, and I am loath to keep on throwing good money after bad, and try other recipes from this book, even those where the reviews on here support their successful outcomes. I think I will stick to my tried and tested Delia, Nigella and Jamie recipe books. I have asked Lorraine via her Facebook page for confirmation of the peanut butter quantity, but so far she has not (nor any of her team) confirmed this, but instead has ignored my question, and prefers to talk about what others are cooking for their evening meals instead. Not impressed.'

While the compliments obviously pleased her, harsh comments really stung. For Lorraine had worked her way up into the court of 'celebrity chef' through a combination of need and self-survival, as well as the more orthodox path of professional training and experience. But there are still some cynics who will always sneer at the success of a beautiful woman who switched between such diverse careers. Said Lorraine: 'I've always wanted to do something creative, something I could put everything into. I fell into modelling and it was a job where I was the product. It was all about my appearance rather than anything I'd produced or made myself. Now I love what I do so much and I'm really proud that I've built it up from scratch. If people are enjoying the TV programme and finding me accessible, it's brilliant. I'm just being myself and I hope people can see my passion.'

Fortunately, most of the aspiring cooks and books reviewers shared that passion and loved *Baking Made Easy*:

'I have this book after seeing her programme on BBC2. At first I wasn't warmed to her but I gradually like her style of baking and [she seemed] honest.'

'I enjoyed her book. So far I have made Doris Grant loaf, a big hit in my household, delicious when eaten straight out of the oven. You MUST try the Camembert cheese with roasted garlic, nom nom.'

'Saw the TV series and thought I'd get the book to see just how easy it was. The recipes are simple to follow and so far everything I've made has been a success and has tasted great.'

'Very rarely a cook book is so well written. The recipes are flawless, coherent and if followed correctly the final product is perfect every time. I have enjoyed learning new techniques and skills.'

'I like baking. I am not good at it and was looking for some easy recipes and instructions. After seeing Lorraine on TV and being impressed and inspired by what I saw, I bought the book and was not disappointed. I would and do recommend it to anyone.'

It was this majority of fans of the new BBC2 'home baking heroine' which kept *Baking Made Easy* (often seen casually lying around Lorraine's TV kitchen and caught on camera) in the bestseller list. 'In this gorgeous new cook book to accompany the series Lorraine shares her expertise, passion and her all-time favourite sweet and savoury recipes. Baking is back and as a qualified baker with years of experience in some of the country's hottest restaurants, Lorraine knows just how to create modern, delicious and inspiring recipes.' The book was eventually reprinted four times and was still at number 17 in Amazon's rankings two years later.

Fans also clamoured to find out what they should buy to compete with 'Beautiful Baker Girl' Lorraine's baking skills – for reference she has said her kitchen 'musts' are a Salter digital timer with a loud alarm – 'so I can concentrate on other tasks safe in the knowledge that I'll be alerted when the food in my oven is ready', stainless steel portioners (mechanical ice-cream serving scoops) – 'I use them in increasing sizes for cookies and cupcakes', a ProCook cooling rack – 'avoid stacking cooling racks if you use them for cakes as the upper layers can go soggy due to the steaming effect,' and on her cookery programmes she uses a KitchenAid Artisan stand mixer in brushed nickel – 'available at many places online'.

(One appearance of the KitchenAid prompted an

excited 'tweet'. 'Watching Lorraine Pascale use her KitchenAid mixer and pasta attachment on tonight's *Home Cooking Made Easy* on BBC2. Looks delicious!' The tweet was from KitchenAid. Lorraine was fast becoming an advertiser's dream. One electrical site hailed this piece of kitchen equipment as 'a seriously cool looking appliance with its retro design and cutting edge technology making it a culinary must have. Lorraine Pascale has one in pearlescent metallic. If you want to make a Tiramisu cake like Lorraine, it is easy to do with a KitchenAid stand mixer.'

Lorraine's use of a Salter Magic Lens Electronic Scale also prompted her fans to invest in the same. 'I'd seen Lorraine Pascale using one like this and was delighted when mine arrived and proved to be every bit as good as promised.' (There would no doubt be a surge in Breville slow cookers after Lorraine bought a £14.99 one from Sainsbury's in early 2012, 'and it comes in red, my favourite colour.') In fact there was something of a 'Lorraine Factor' with sales of certain cooking items and home-baking equipment soaring. There were milk chocolate cigarillos 'as seen on Lorraine Pascale's *Baking Made Easy*', piping bags – 'Having determined to have a go at Lorraine Pascale's stunning Crouching Tiger, Hidden Zebra cake, I had to find large piping bags that could be knotted at the top end. These are just perfect!' – plus a host of 'Lorraine' products.

Newspapers made great play of the fact that bakeware sales had doubled and that 'decorating and icing products are up by about 70 per cent'. The figures came from a report by consumer research group Mintel which estimated that 28 per cent of people in the UK now bake from scratch using raw ingredients every week. Further, John Lewis reported that sales of its mixing bowls were up by 40 per cent, its cupcake sales up a whopping 305 per cent and its cake tin range and other baking equipment was up 21 per cent. Kitchenware retailer Lakeland also said that it had experienced an increase in sales of its bakeware items which was attributed to the growing trend of 'homemade is best' especially in 'areas such as cupcakes'.

Victoria Summerley wrote in the *Independent*: 'Behind this boom in baking is a new generation – raised on celebrity chefs' best-selling books and ratings-grabbing television shows – that is spending more time in the kitchen. The recession-inspired zeitgeist for "make do and mend" only adds to the trend.' That same month, it was also reported that Lorraine's sweet ideas were behind a boost in sales of icing sugar (well, its ready-to-roll icing packs to be factual) at upmarket supermarket Waitrose, which were up by 40 per cent. (Romantics keen to cook up creamy delights for their loved ones on Valentine's Day helped increase the sugar surge.) Across all the supermarkets it was noted that flour sales shot up too by 20 per cent as women rediscovered the art of baking.

By simply mentioning a product Lorraine seemed to help boost its popularity no end. Prestigious oven company Neff was one of the benefactors of this in 2012 when it launched its 'Bake it Yourself' site on Facebook to celebrate 40 years of the company being 'at the top in the UK'. The Recommended Agency Register behind the idea was proud to claim: 'It is hard to decide whether the icing on the cake (so far) has been the sales leads given to Neff, the campaign mentions by Lorraine Pascale, the 35,000 who participated in our "What Kind of Baker Are You?" app or securing Andi Peters and *Little Paris Kitchen*'s Rachel Khoo as celebrity fans. Either way we feel like we have had our cake, and eaten it, on this flan-tastic social brief'.

But proving that home baking – definitely Lorraine's signature tag – really had stirred the nation to have a go, the 'Bake it Yourself' page attracted an average of 500 people a day. At the end of six months nearly a million 'likes' were logged. Four million 'hits' were recorded in just one week through viral messages. This was indeed a great publicity success for Neff. What they thought of a sharp-eyed observer noting that Lorraine used hobs and an oven made by Siemens is not recorded.

But in short, Lorraine, new to our screens, had caused a bit of a stir in the kitchen.

Her first series ended on 14 February 2011. It had been hard work, with as many as 15 cakes a day being made – though with most references to Lorraine involving the word 'cupcake' it is easy to forget that she is an expert savoury chef too, despite her programmes featuring a variety of recipes. But she does confess that when it comes to sweet-tooth offerings, she's somewhat biased. 'I like to cook savoury too – but I don't love it in the same way. There's something so comforting about cakes. The smell, the making of it. The eating. Everyone always goes, "Wow!" when you bring a cake to the table. Everyone says, "Oh – just a little bit then! Just a little bit!"'

The pressures of these debut programmes saw Lorraine deliberately staying out of the kitchen for a couple of months after the series ended to give herself a break, to avoid feeling jaded by it all – and to have a rest from the massive amounts of washing up she had had to undertake at the end of each filming session! But there was still some promotional work to under-take, including a demonstration of recipes from *Baking Made Easy* at Waterstones flagship bookstore in Piccadilly, London, on 30 March. (Work commitments saw Lorraine reluctantly pull out of a book signing at Canary Wharf on 24 March.)

Despite the mixed – but mainly favourable – reviews, and wearing what was to become her trademark pristine white T-shirts and long-sleeved shirts (bought from All Saints, Gap and H&M) and changed up to five times during each recording, she was hailed as the BBC's new golden girl of the kitchen. Her BBC2 Monday night show attracted nearly three million viewers, who rather took to the stunning cook with an infectious smile and the descriptions of her 'pillowy' meringues and 'squishy' Swiss rolls, which she prepared with such enthusiasm and passion. People also marvelled at how someone who seemed to spend most of her time concocting high-calorie cakes and dishes rich with cream and other fattening ingredients remained whippet thin.

The series was repeated on the Cooking Channel in October that year under the title *Simply Baking* – 'A cooking and publishing phenomenon, Lorraine Pascale is a unique talent. Her relaxed nature and happy, welcoming style are unrivalled in her field.' The channel was to screen her follow-up series too. It was an exciting and rewarding start to her new career, and although anxious about public reaction, Lorraine felt she had achieved a very important goal. 'After all the sacrifices I've made over so many years it feels exciting to have finally tasted the first bite of what I hope will be the start of a really exciting chapter for me.'

By the middle of 2011 Lorraine was certainly not going unnoticed. She had already been hailed as one of the newest 'young, hot, super-talented culinary queens' in a 'Summer Social' feature in the *Sunday Times Style Magazine* in the summer of 2010, which had Lorraine seated with a selection of other female cooks around a picnic table with food writer Lucas Hollweg in the centre. She was, it said, showing that it was time for '"macho chefs" to move over because there's a whole new breed of cook in town...'

It seemed that Lorraine could do no wrong when it came to supermodel turned supercook, but despite a report in July 2011 that she was to become the new face of Sainsbury's, replacing fellow TV chef Jamie Oliver and thus ending his 11-year association with the supermarket chain, neither Sainsbury's nor Lorraine's 'people' would comment. Wherever the rumour came from – it may have been fuelled by the fact that Sainsbury's boss Justin King was the UK managing director of Häagen-Dazs when Lorraine was hired for the infamous 'Lose Control' adverts – plus the claim that Sainsbury's was 'keen to finalise a deal with Miss Pascale', the link-up did not happen. Though she did later sign up with Waitrose to write a column for its magazine, *Waitrose Food Illustrated*. It was clear that Lorraine was hot property.

Chapter 9

Second helpings

Lorraine's second TV series began on 26 September 2011. Under the umbrella title *Home Cooking Made Easy*, it was in four parts – 'Comfort' ('For dinner Lorraine thinks that after a hard day nothing beats five-spice baked ribs with a sticky honey sesame sauce'), 'Favourites' ('She cranks up the volume on a kitchen classic with a prosciutto and brie toastie that's ready in moments'), 'Entertaining' ('Staying in is the new going out, and Lorraine has got entertaining at home covered') and 'Simple' ('Lorraine Pascale's food series comes to a delicious finale with an episode that is all about simple, scrumptious recipes that will knock people's socks off').

The first programme of the series attracted more than 2.5m viewers, beating BBC1's *Panorama*. It also prompted a somewhat chauvinistic review from the *Guardian*'s Sam Wollaston: 'So what's Lorraine Pascale's USP, apart from the fact that she's named after a quiche? Her winning smile, I think. It's absolutely lovely. All of her is, to be honest, she's very, very pretty – about a billion times more so than Gregg from *MasterChef*. So pretty that before she was a TV chef she used to be a top model. What are we going to learn to make, then? I'm thinking minimal, probably, a big white plate with three pale strips on it: one stick of celery, one line of coke, one cigarette. Mmmm. With a flute of Moët to wash it down, and some kind of diuretic pill or laxative for afters. Oh, quite the opposite…That means chocolate marshmallow fudge which involves melting together a load of butter, evaporated milk, sugar, chocolate and marshmallows into a big, hyper-calorific, artery-clogging gloop. God that looks disgusting. And look at you, Lorraine, and look at that – I don't believe you've ever had more than the tiniest nibble of this stuff. There's nothing to inspire me here, no recipes I'd want to tear out if they were in a magazine. The only thing I would like to tear out here is the host (he says, increasingly seedily). She sits on the steps, alliterative in her pink pashmina, pouting about pasta, Parmesan, and pancetta, mmmm … stop it!'

And a review in the *Daily Mirror* also raised the big question once again about how such a calorific cook could be so slim:

'Every TV chef has an angle. Nigella's got sauce, Heston's got his laboratory. Lorraine Pascale's angle is that her food has magically had all the calories removed. It must have done. How else can she cook like this and look like that? We first met former model Lorraine when she presented *Baking Made Easy*. Now she's telling us that life isn't too short to roll our own tagliatelle – and this may well be the first time a wire coat hanger has featured as a kitchen utensil. There'd be a run on them in Tesco tomorrow if we didn't already have wardrobes full of wire hangers we're desperate to get rid of.

'As it turns out, Lorraine's pasta with cream and pancetta is the least fattening thing on the menu. Her theme this week is comfort food – and we're talking about the kind of comfort that comes from layers and layers of padding and leaves you looking like a well-lagged boiler.

'We see Lorraine tucking into home-made chocolate marshmallow fudge and, for pudding, she makes a cake by lining a bowl with slices of shop-bought Swiss roll and then filling it with four or five tubs of expensive chocolate ice cream.

'Seriously. Lorraine's wasted presenting cookery programmes. Any fool can cook. What we really need to know is how to eat chocolate ice cream and Swiss roll and look half as good as she does.'

The accompanying *Home Cooking Made Easy* book was released on 29 September – 'The queen of cookery is back with 100 scrumptious and seriously easy recipes, from cosy soups and roasts to delicious autumnal breads, in this beautifully photographed second book'.

Again, most of the reviews from keen cooks were favourable:

'I bought this book as soon as I heard about it as I bought Lorraine's previous book *Baking Made Easy* and this one is just as good. The recipes are easy and simple to follow – the photographs stunning – making me want to try each recipe as I turn the pages over. Was not sure if the 21st Century Bread would work without yeast but I was not disappointed – it was lovely. If like me you are a simple cook – liking uncomplicated recipes – then this is the book for you.'

'This has to be one of the best cookery books around at the moment, really enjoyed the series and the book compliments it well, lovely recipes and easy to follow. Had to buy the *Baking Made Easy* too. Fabulous books !!'

'As a mum of three hard-to-please children, I've been delighted with the positive responses from all the family. So far I've made the quick brown sugar and spring onion chicken teriyaki, the creamy pancetta pasta, the paprika baked fish, the mini beef Wellingtons (for hubby and me), the not-so-slow lamb, and the caramelised banana bread and butter pudding. They have all been a success. I don't think I've ever bought a cookbook (I have over 100) and wanted to cook so many things from it. The recipes are straightforward and easy to put together and cook, with lots of flavour and are also easily adaptable for fussy or more adventurous eaters – I can't wait to make more from it.'

This time the harsher criticism was aimed at what readers felt was a lack of detail when preparing some of the dishes, omissions over measurements and basic errors:

'I haven't cooked much from this book yet – the recipes I have done have been fine, BUT I'm not sure whether an editor has been anywhere near this book. One recipe calls for the oven to be preheated, but it's never actually used in the recipe. Another asks you to fry some potatoes and set them aside, but they are never added to the final dish. And those are just the ones I've noticed so far. Perhaps watching the series was essential to understanding the book. I don't doubt the ability of the chef, but the book is not brilliantly put-together, meaning you have to guess a few of the steps. Personally, as a disliker-of-pears, I find there are far too many recipes which contain pears.'

'There are definitely some inaccuracies in this book. I tried to do the chocolate steamed pudding with sauce and every time I melted Mars bars, they just split and I wasted about nine Mars bars in the end. Also the lamb shank recipe says to add a whole sausage, which is ridiculous. In the picture, they are quite clearly sliced, which is what I did in the end. Great book but you do need to fill in the gaps on a few occasions.'

'Although I love the recipes in this book, the editor should have been shot. There are some errors with measures, which have left me with a few kitchen disasters. Also there should be more pictures of the finished food than of her.'

Lorraine, a stickler for detail to the point of being obsessive when it comes to ensuring everything with her name on it is perfect, must have been mortified by the glitches that these few readers complained about. But they were greatly outweighed by the glowing reviews from more than satisfied followers, who pronounced 'I love Lorraine'.

She was now garnering interest from other quarters too. One group finding inspiration through Lorraine's success was Blackerprise – 'promoting successful micro-entrepreneurship within the black community' – which gave this stirring piece of advice on its internet site on 11 October 2011: 'Be your own person. Know what you want and work at getting it. Don't settle for something you don't like because it is working. A lot of people would have said Lorraine was crazy to leave a successful modelling career but she did. Why? Because she knew this wasn't the life she wanted. Do you know what you want? If you do then why are you not going for it? What's holding you back? What are you scared of? Yes, we don't like change and prefer to stick with what is comfortable, but life is much more exciting when you step out of your comfort zone to seek out what you are passionate about.'

Another online magazine site, All Black Woman – for 'intelligent black women' – echoed the praise for someone who had made it despite the challenges, saying she had 'perfect excuses to be bitter and angry about life. But not Lorraine, she refused to let her past become a handicap. Of course one must not forget the fact that her adoptive parents were very caring and have been very supportive in her journey towards who she is today. Nevertheless one has to admire her courage for achieving what she has despite the challenging background she had.' Lorraine, it was noted, was 'not your everyday woman.'

Also in October 2011, charity TACT – The Adolescent and Children's Trust – announced that Lorraine had become its first celebrity patron. She had supported the group since January that year. A spokesman said: 'We are honoured that she has now decided to champion our charity in this way. As a care leaver and adopted child herself, Lorraine knows only too well the issues a child in care faces. Lorraine now hopes to use her personal experiences to positively promote the plight of looked after children alongside TACT's work.' The Trust's chief executive Kevin Williams added: 'We are honoured that Lorraine has decided to champion our charity. Her achievements are a glowing example of how children who have been in care can achieve their dreams and flourish.'

For Lorraine, it was a case of promoting the issues faced by children in care, and the charity was certainly dear to her heart. Its core work was originally the provision of foster placements for children in the care of local authorities. The group later merged with the Independent Adoption Services and joined together with the charity Parents for Children. TACT's mission has been to provide effective services and to campaign on behalf of children and young people in care and families. 'Everything we do is for the benefit of children in care and on the fringes of care,' its website states.

For Lorraine, her mission was simple: 'I am passionate about kids coming out of care,' she has said. 'I love the work that TACT does.' Lorraine now works with the charity in a bid to try to increase the number of families who can adopt. Showing her commitment to the charity, she aimed to raise £2,000 from the 10k London Run she took part in on 8 July 2012 (she raised much more, having reached over £3,000 of pledges by the day of the race, for a final total of £3,295). Lorraine had lots of support from family, friends and fans, with a generous £100 sponsorship from 'rival' glamorous TV cook Nigella Lawson and the message 'Good Luck', £50 from model agency Storm, £150 from fitness guru Jonathan Lomax and £150 from agents James Grant Media, as well as £20 from her brother Jason, £50 from her dad Roger and £20 from step-mum Katie – with the words 'We're so proud of you.'

Lorraine, in a bright pink TACT vest (she was given the race number 9993) and navy baseball cap, tweeted pictures of her efforts throughout the day. Afterwards it was early to bed with a book and a pot of chamomile tea. But despite the aches and pains she was already planning her next fund-raiser...

Lorraine also runs cookery sessions for children in

care and families. And there is a more personal element to this. She is very conscious of missing some of the basic school subjects because of her transient childhood. She said: 'For me, it was not getting a good education in grammar, for instance. For these children it is not having cookery lessons. It's about teaching them a few basic skills.'

Lorraine also teaches cooking for the Barnardo's children's charity – 'I want to get hands-on involved, not just with some fabulous party opening thing.' Of course she is also aware of the importance of having someone who shows an interest in you. Sometimes being in care means a child can miss out on having one-to-one relationships with a parent figure. 'I always think that children in that environment, if you have just one person you can talk to, who can be there when you're going through all the rubbish, it can really save you.' Poignantly, too she has commented: 'I don't think cooking sees colour...'

Lorraine's successful 2011 ended with her hour-long BBC2 programme, *Lorraine's Last Minute Christmas*, in which she gave her own 'special tips on how to create a perfect celebratory dinner at short notice. From ordering food over the internet to creating the perfect Christmas gift hamper and making the most of leftovers, Lorraine tells us everything we need to know about getting food on the table and culinary gifts under the tree with minimum cost and fuss.'

But again she could not please everyone. In the *Independent* Alice-Azania Jarvis wrote: 'Evidently, Lorraine Pascale has graduated. She is now so sufficiently recognised, enough of a household name, that she's Lorraine... and so it was that we were treated to *Lorraine's Last Minute Christmas*, complete with mince pie stars, stained-glass cookies and Lorraine in reindeer slippers. And if you can possibly bear to pay attention to any more Christmas cooking shows, this one had some useful tips. There was a nice segment on affordable wines, and a moderately informative chat with a butcher about what to cook for two, and whether you can still find turkey on Christmas Eve. There was also a truly horrendous-looking winter wonderland Christmas tray bake. In fact, if you are in the market for festive advice, here's mine. Don't, for the love of God, make that.'

Unfortunately, there were still the rather unpleasant Lorraine watchers who used the internet to post less than constructive criticism. Sometimes it would come out of the blue and sometimes it would follow one of Lorraine's TV programmes. But always it came from the less educated, less eloquent and those generally far-removed from the more normal critical public. On 12 January 2012, someone calling themselves Kinky Melinky wrote on RedCafe.net: 'I realise she's physically attractive but she's as annoying as fuck.'

'CassiusClaymore' responded: 'I disagree Kinky. I

adore her cheeky gap-toothed smile and love the way she sniffs in every dish she's cooked as if God himself had broken wind...'

Luckily, such exchanges are restricted to minority forums.

But being one of a number of celebrity chefs on TV will always mean comparisons with your contemporaries. And Lorraine was no exception. Several newspapers carried 'who is best?' articles. These often blurred a straightforward, reasoned critique of cooking skills with more personal assessments.

Sunday Times food editor Hilary Biller wrote one such piece on 24 April 2012: 'On TV she's natural, charming, unpretentious, un-smug about her perfect kitchen, perfect cooking, perfect life. You want to eat her food, be her friend, have her lovely smooth skin (some personal aspects of the 90s really will haunt me forever). She cooks easy food that looks almost as scrummy as her, serving it up at the end of each episode to a couple of pals, a less raucous and more current version of Jamie O. Anyone who adds gorgonzola and breadcrumbs to pasta and calls it "Glam Mac and Cheese" is alright in my book.'

On 27 April 2012 the *Guardian* ran an article comparing the merits of Lorraine with those of fellow easy-on-the-eye cooks Gizzi Erskine and Rachel Khoo. Of course, being a glamorous TV chef means being at the mercy of style-watchers ever ready to give their view on both. The *Guardian* feature described Lorraine's style as resembling more of a 'preppy J Crew catalogue model than a sweaty chef... her wardrobe pushes the ex-model shtick too: bright sweaters, white shirts and jeans. It's unthreatening and wholesome and made her the darling of glossy women's mags. Refreshing as it is that Pascale has eschewed the 1950s housewife thing, her athletic, vitamin-enriched look is misleading – there's no way you'll look that good if you try to emulate her baking expertise. She acquires certificates the way other chefs acquire stove burns (as well as the Leiths Diploma, she has a first in Culinary Arts Management and an International Culinary Arts degree), but it's her devotion to the cupcake that triggered her ascent to celebrity chefdom.' This was followed by the recipe for Lorraine's 'I Can't Believe You Made That' cake.

There was, too, the comparison with fellow former model Sophie Dahl, who had burst onto the TV screens with her cookery programme *The Delicious Miss Dahl* in April 2010. Lorraine was also included in a 'four stylish TV chefs' article alongside Gizzi Erskine, Rachel Khoo and Nigella Lawson. Writer Gemma Lucy Press commented that 'not only do these four ladies create some of the most mouth-wateringly good (or bad depending on your views on calorific food) dishes, but they also do it with such style, such flair and such damn good dress sense. I know it may seem odd to be taking clothing tips from chefs but these girls really do know how to dress. They're real women whose passion for food has put them in the spotlight, so they dress like real women, but with their own unique and scrumptious style.'

Of Lorraine, Press said: 'Being an ex-model you'd question Lorraine's love of oh-so-good-but-seriously-it's-bad-for-you-food, but it's genuine. From reading her books you can tell she's had a great relationship with food.'

Lorraine is used to being discussed in terms of how she squares up against her TV 'rivals' – with Jamie Oliver and Nigella Lawson being the two most usually cited in any comparisons. 'But I've been called the new everyone really,' she has said. 'Apart from Gordon Ramsay. No one has tried to compare him to me.' Is that because she doesn't go in for Ramsay's more, shall we say, aggressive approach to kitchen discipline? Joked Lorraine: 'Obviously, they haven't heard my language when I'm in the car...'

But if critics like to compare Lorraine with other chefs, she herself certainly doesn't. In fact she makes a point of not 'looking at what other chefs do' and does not read their books or watch their TV programmes for inspiration, preferring to do her 'own thing'. If pressed, however, she will admit to *Iron Chef America*, as well as *MasterChef Australia* being her favourite programmes – and good old Mrs Beeton as one of her favourite cooks.

Those who might have missed Lorraine's appearances on *Saturday Kitchen* first time around had the chance to catch up on a 'best bites' segment of the programme later that year. She appeared in 12 repeated 'best bites' between 15 April and 6 October in 2012. And her Monday night programmes were repeated after *Saturday Kitchen* on Saturday mornings at 11.30am, meaning Lorraine fans had a double weekend serving of her for a while. In between all this was a 40-second promotional film for Lorraine's upcoming new *Fast, Fresh and Easy Food* series. The trailer is interesting for several reasons. It appears on several chef's websites, has the added tease of a 'see how many chefs you can spot?', a voiceover extolling the virtues of cooking – 'food is a celebration that comes out of nowhere...' and a selection of some of TV's most popular chefs when they were children and in their younger days. There are three photographs of Lorraine, one when she was aged five, one as she is today, and a rare snapshot of her sitting on a beach with her teenage Afro hair.

In August, Lorraine flew to America on business but she took some time out to relax too. One of her activities was a trip to the cinema to see 'something gritty and real to counterbalance the wonderfully heady showbiz world that is Los Angeles!' The film she saw was *Take This Waltz* (about a married man's affair) and Lorraine posted a review. Rather poignantly, it touched on her own failed marriage. 'It revolves around a happily married couple seemingly very much in love, caught in the tedium of everyday life. But then, as in so many relationships, the challenge of temptation arrives – and with it an all-encompassing reminder of how it feels to be lustful, captivated and excited with another once more. What would you do? *Take This Waltz* is definitely worth a watch. It's not a Hollywood blockbuster or a predictable rom-com but an intelligent, sympathetic flick that provokes thought and reflection...'

Chapter 10

Going global

Lorraine's third series, *Fast, Fresh and Easy Food*, aired for six weeks from 13 August to 17 September 2012. There was 'Easy Entertaining' ('Lorraine Pascale creates food that is perfect for when friends turn up out of the blue'), 'Feel Good Food' ('Lorraine creates the kind of dishes that put a smile on your face'), 'Simple Classics' ('Lorraine demonstrates how to create classic dishes with minimum effort'), 'Baking It' ('Lorraine indulges in her passion for baking and reveals some quick and simple ideas'), 'Posh Nosh' ('Lorraine turns her attention to some seriously posh nosh that is guaranteed to impress') and 'Everyday Easy'

('Lorraine turns her attention to those quick-fix meals that need to fit into everyday life').

Again, viewers aired their opinions – and most were still smitten:

'Lorraine Pascale has made a name for herself presenting recipes that are tasty, attractive on the plate and accessible. This is not some three-star chef preparing lobster terrine in ways that make the average home chef pull their hair out in exasperation. Her cooking is appealing because it is within the reach of people who won't be producing intricate food that requires the dedication of a surgeon to get right.'

'She is one of my favourite TV chefs because the meals she makes are unpretentious yet delicious. I love watching her on TV because she comes across as so genuinely smiley and happy and you get the feeling that she would be a really good friend to have. I love her recipes for steak and spicy pasta most.'

'Some good ideas and a few things I will certainly be making but I think the main problem is that the TV show has failed to inspire me this time around. The filming style is different and much more about the process of making the recipes than the personality of the hostess convincing you of the merits of the dish and why it's so good. I like that personal touch and a bit of a story, not just a how-to video.'

And by now, viewers were even asking what music was played to accompany the preparation and triumphant completion of the various dishes Lorraine cooked on television:

'Hi, just as you start to make the Neti bread and before Emeli Sandé starts to play, there is a piece of music heavy with guitar that is playing – what is it, please?'

'Hi, what is the music that is playing right at the start when you talk about the things you are going to cook? It is driving me crazy! Thank you :)'

The BBC obliged by providing a week-by-week full running list of all the songs on Lorraine's website.

And Lorraine herself took to her official website to announce how wonderful it all was. 'Filming the show was oodles of fun. The crew made me feel so comfortable and I really looked forward to going to work in the mornings, which is always a great feeling! It has been a sincere labour of love and both the book and the show are something that I am totally passionate about. I feel really blessed that I get the chance to do what I love best – and get paid for it!'

There had been one small hiccup during the series, however. Somehow the wrong quantities for one of her recipes, Crouching Tiger, Hidden Zebra cake, were given on the TV programme. Lorraine made an apology to one baffled mother on mumsnet who said her cake did not turn out as she had expected: 'It took a lot longer to cook through, leaving overdone edges and the centre rose'. Lorraine confessed that when she is doing her programmes the ingredients are weighed out for her 'so I can focus on presenting.' She said she had been given the wrong quantities for this particular recipe 'and may have then said incorrect weights.' Lorraine politely apologised for wasting the mum's time. The BBC also later changed the recipe on its iPlayer.

This time the accompanying book of the series was published on the day of the first episode, 13 August, with Lorraine saying her aim on this occasion was to 'encourage people to cook from fresh in busy lives... those who, like me and my family, face the same daily dilemma of "What on earth is for dinner?" The goal of *Fast, Fresh and Easy Food* was to create something people would revisit time and again. A cookbook that would be on the kitchen counter several times a week, for busy people who love good food and want to make something quick and easy. And I wanted to provide an entire meal, main dish and side. So often when you know what you want to cook, it is challenging to figure out what to have with it. Within this book, I have served up dishes with an accompaniment or two, making meals much easier to plan. I also tried to make it as simple as possible so that everything is served up together, with a time plan for each recipe so you can sail through the instructions and end up with a delicious dish in super-fast time. I wrote this book for me and my family and for you and your family, and hope that it helps you to serve up fresh, fast and delicious meals every day.' But as ever, while Lorraine was pretty pleased with the book she had spent sleepless nights and hectic days compiling, still there was a handful of dissatisfied customers. This time everything from Lorraine's Chicken Tikka to teaspoon measurements; photographs to fuzzy print was focused on:

'I bought this book on my Kindle as I have millions of cookery books. First of all let me say that some of the print is quite light grey and therefore makes it difficult to read. Anyway, I decided to make the little jammy tarts as I'd seen Lorraine do on the TV. I measured everything accurately but you know what, the jam in the bottom of each tart bubbled over and made a mess of the pastry and stuck the tarts to the tin. Maybe she should have put "teaspoon" instead of "tablespoon". What a performance trying to get them out! I hope the rest of her recipes turn out a bit better than this.'

'I bought Lorraine's book after watching her TV programme and when she made her take on Chicken Tikka Masala it gave me the nudge to get it. Well, I have to say this is the worst Chicken Tikka I have ever had. I am so disappointed. It's just such a waste of ingredients, time, and effort, and it also makes me wonder if these recipes have been tested. The recipe states 200g tomato puree – that's an awful lot, so thank goodness for Amazon I am able to send this book back.'

'The photography is decidedly average with none of the verve and "make-me appeal" of the TV programme. Ms Pascale is ill-served by her publishers here; check out the Waitrose monthly food mag, Lorraine – that's the kind of "must-make-this" quality of photography you need – and deserve!'

Meanwhile, a review in the *Metro* hinted that it might take longer to make Lorraine's dishes than one anticipated: 'Beware. Following the directions, it's not possible to produce the five-spice roasted duck with cherry and Shiraz sauce and sesame noodles in the advertised 15 minutes, and it'll only feed four if two of you don't like noodles. It tastes great, though – and that's as good a way to cheer up a midweek dinner as any.'

One eagle-eyed reviewer was also quick to point out that Lorraine's 'Lazza's Lamb Biryani' recipe was missing a few instructions: 'I realised that the recipe is indeed unfinished and the reader/cook is left abandoned with browned meat. She turns her attention to cooking coconut rice pumped up with sundried tomatoes and herbs and the meat is never again mentioned in the dish.'

A review in the *Cork Independent* on 17 November did end on a better and rather fond note, though: 'The fact that there is a half-finished recipe in Lorraine Pascale's *Fast, Fresh and Easy Food* only endears me to her further. I'm often asked which cooks I like and what cookbooks I use and Jamie will always feature among my favourites, along with Nigel Slater who is the food writing Deity in my opinion, and now Lorraine is up there too. They are my Culinary Trinity at the moment. I am loving Lorraine for her practicality and oneness with us "normal" people. What other chef would admit to this: "I am not at all embarrassed to say that on many occasions I have returned home to the waiting party laden with food that just needs a simple peeling back of the plastic and a slight turn of the oven dial." Three cheers for Lorraine, I love her.'

Fervent Lorraine fans and followers amongst the general public expressed similar feelings:

'We love Lorraine Pascale in our house, her programmes are interesting and up to date and not too complicated like some chefs and the book is just the same. Everything is set out and explained really well and not too fancy or fussy. You could quite easily and happily cook everything in the book, it doesn't contain any overly fancy things, once again like some chefs who cook things that the average person wouldn't dream of or be able to cook, with ingredients that you'd never find only in specialist shops. Usually you have to leaf through these books and find just a few things you could do, but Lorraine's recipes aren't like that at all. She makes everything look so simple and actually seems to really enjoy all that she cooks and uses ingredients that are easy to obtain, sometimes making welcome shortcuts. We have all her books and find them all as interesting. My husband is the main cook in our house and he's cooked loads of her recipes and reckons she's the best cook book writer of them all.'

'I think Lorraine's new book is absolutely brilliant. I'm recommending it to all my friends. The recipes are amazing and I love the fact that she gives you suggestions for complete meals and then takes you through the whole meal step by step in the recipe. I've only had the book a few days but I've cooked with it every single night and can't wait to have more time with it over the weekend.'

There was further recognition of Lorraine's talents when she was listed as being one of the 'culinary masters' (alongside Jamie Oliver and Rick Stein) on the write club website, which said: 'A slightly controversial choice but a fully justified one. There is no doubt that a huge part of the appeal of a dish is its visual impact, and Miss Pascale is light years ahead of her contemporaries when it comes to aesthetically pleasing plates of food. She claims (as all TV chefs do) to make food "easy". Whether that is true or not is open to debate, but there can be no such argument when it comes to her ability to produce cakes and pastries that look genuinely stunning.'

The overwhelming positive reaction to Lorraine's books certainly impressed her publisher. Based very much on the fact that they had already reaped more than £4.4m in sales in Britain alone, HarperCollins signed a new three-book deal with Lorraine in April 2012, a commitment to two more books after *Fast, Fresh and Easy Food*. Said HarperCollins chief executive Victoria Barnsley: 'We have huge plans to help her reach the next level as she joins the ranks of global cookery brands.' World rights were bought by Harper non-fiction publisher Carole Tonkins from Nicola Ibison, head of the Factual and Current Affairs Division at Lorraine's management company, James Grant.

Lorraine does not give many 'live' interviews – she has never done a TV chat show – but she has talked several times on radio to promote her books and display her cooking skills to her hosts. The first of these appearances was on 12 January 2011 when she was a discussion guest on Radio 4's *Midweek: Diverse Conversation* programme hosted by Libby Purves. It was here that she talked about her eating habits during her modelling days, the decision to give it all up and the path that led her to becoming a chef. Purves described Lorraine as 'shining and irrepressible, zooming around on a scooter'. The next radio talks were to promote *Fast, Fresh and Easy Food* and the most personal of these was on Radio 4's *Woman's Hour* on 2 October 2012, when she spoke about her links with Barnardo's, her own adoption and being 'discovered' by a model scout.

Lorraine's appearance on *The Graham Norton Show* on Radio 2 a week or so earlier was much more light-hearted – and centred very much around food. In fact Lorraine pulled out all the stops. She had prepared a special menu for Norton, started cooking at 8am and despite one small disaster – when she burned the butter in her peanut butter squares – had completed everything by 9.15am. Proving just what a down-to-earth girl she is, Lorraine had ventured out to buy her ingredients wearing her favourite comfy Ugg boots and a coat on top of her pyjamas. And she did the same as she went out again to purchase replacement ingredients for the burned bits! But it all came good in the end and Lorraine was able to present Norton with perfect peanut butter squares, pancetta and blueberry and oat muffins. All this and she even had time to fit in a hairdresser's appointment at 9.45am!

Lorraine was back on Radio 4 on 6 October on *Weekend Woman's Hour* when she created the 'perfect chocolate mousse' – perfected by the use of 'fresh eggs bought on the day you need them', an electric hand whisk and 'good-quality chocolate'. And there were other guest spots on local radio stations including BBC Radio Lincolnshire.

Fast, Fresh and Easy Food was nominated for an award in the Food and Drink category of the Specsavers National Book of Awards. Two days before the awards ceremony Lorraine was at the Aalto Restaurant at Birmingham's Hotel La Tour to showcase some of the recipes from her book and to host a dinner party alongside the brasserie's lead chef Dan Pearce, who seemed more than happy to cook with the TV chef. 'It's always a pleasure to be able to showcase our restaurant and kitchen. It was great to meet Lorraine and talk to her about her style of cooking. She prepared the starter and chatted to the guests, talking about her love of food.' Ten winners of a competition run by radio's Heart FM were invited guests. The main course and dessert were chosen by Lorraine and were from the à la carte menu at Aalto. Foodies might like to know the full menu:

Crunchy black pepper halloumi dip sticks with a spicy harissa hummus, served with Saint Cosme Côtes du Rhône;

Slow-braised pork cheeks, lentils and sage, mash and red cabbage, served with Altas de Ruesca, Garnacha, Spain;

Pear and almond tart with clotted cream, served with sparkling Rosa Regale from Tuscan vineyard Banfi.

It was a busy weekend for Lorraine as she had also made an appearance at the BBC Good Food Show there.

Sadly Lorraine's *Fast, Fresh and Easy Food* did not win the WH Smith-sponsored Food and Drink category at the ceremony held on 4 December at London's Mandarin Oriental Hotel (one of her old training grounds). She was pipped to the post by TV's bearded biking cooks, Simon King and Dave Myers, and their book, *The Hairy Dieters.*

Meanwhile, the ever present – and not always wholly constructive – TV-watching critics were ranting on both mainstream and slightly more obscure sites. A reviewer on the giddy kipper website wrote:

'I love cooking... I'm not massive on baking. But I don't think you need to be both. And I think perhaps that's a lesson Lorraine Pascale might want to learn. The model-turned-cake maker has also, somehow, managed to turn herself into a TV chef. Except she's not. Yes, I think she's got a diploma in cooking, but no, I really don't think that qualifies her to share her "recipes" with us on a prime time TV show. Unfortunately, the BBC bosses do, and so I sat down to watch. First up was some strange "one minute pesto" recipe... Take garlic, Parmesan, basil, pine nuts and oil. Whizz them up and there you go... pesto. Seriously?! Does anyone who tunes into a cooking show not know this?! Maybe Lorraine Pascale's show and book (and no, I don't want a copy, thanks), is aimed at people who genuinely have never cooked before. Or maybe it's just a half-hour filler, with Lorraine looking beautiful. Whatever it is, it's not making me very giddy at all!'

Another said: 'I cannot bear this woman. I watched one of her shows in her first series and she sounded like someone who had just been told what half of the ingredients were about half an hour before and was repeating this to camera as though we are all idiots... I gave her another chance with the first episode of the current series and nothing has changed. It seems she makes TV shows for people who have never cooked anything other than a ready meal.'

And it got worse:

'...the worst TV cook ever. Swans around the kitchen activating machines and waffling on about her modelling career and childhood... this is in between scenes of her holding a cup of tea and updating her blog. Crap.'

'I know she's a go-getter – and nice – but she bores me silly.'

If all this wasn't enough Lorraine also had to contend once more with those showing an interest in her cooking programmes for all the wrong reasons. Examples included doctored clips which one assumes were created solely to get the obligatory public airing on the mad and the bad forum of YouTube. Played around with by 'ToxicBarracuda', who no doubt had too much time on his hands, the minute-long film blanked out the start of the word 'baking' spoken several times by Lorraine so that the reference sounded like something more offensive. This somewhat schoolboy humoured TV 'short' also contained blanked-out references to cooking utensils to create sexually suggestive commentary. Fortunately, it seems the 'mastermind' behind it all got bored after this one effort.

Some more tasteful television showings of Lorraine that year, however, came by way of her *Baking Made Easy* series being broadcast in South Africa on BBC Lifestyle SA: 'Already a huge hit in the UK, hot new talent Lorraine Pascale will be making her exclusive debut appearance on South African television this coming spring with her new show *Baking Made Easy*. Lorraine has worked in some of the hottest UK restaurants while simultaneously juggling life as a mother, food journalist and business owner.' The June publicity for the South African showing added that: 'From quick and easy to daring, dazzling and inspiring dishes with a real wow factor, *Baking Made Easy* offers helpful shortcuts and professional kitchen secrets whilst offering large slices of glamour and baking know-how.'

Lorraine's cookery programmes are now shown throughout the world – and each country has its own Pascale following. In Bulgaria and Serbia she appears in a 'Ladies Party' segment with other women boasting various skills, as well as screenings of her series shown in Britain, under the title *24 Kitchen*. Just as in Britain, foreign fans want to air their views. Take

Croatia, for example – where 'lost in translation' idiosyncrasies only add to the charm:

'In a series of known chefs in that channel appeared to me a totally unknown person – Lorraine Pascale. Delighted me at first! Her meals are simple, delicious, imaginative and the fervor with which the story of food could hardly leave anyone indifferent.'

'I've heard of Lorraine but I am not intimately familiar with its work...'

'For some time I prepare to make brownies recipe by LP. Today I tried it, all as specified before I even checked the plunger on YouTube. I did not drop it right, grabbed the cover which is easily broken, and there was a pretty soggy but not in a good way. Where can I stumbled?'

(Perhaps Lorraine found all this endearing too because one of her tweets – on 12 July 2012 – was 'Anyone been to Croatia? What's it like?')

In Turkey, Lorraine is hailed as 'a very popular dish' with 'his very approachable style...'

There was also interest from the Ukraine, with a journalist putting in a special request: 'I'm a big fan of your talent and your show! And also I am a journalist of a Ukrainian daily talk show "Everything will be Fine" (very similar to the Martha Stewart's show). Our show is very popular in Ukraine and especially our viewers love our cookery section of the show. I have a question for you. What do you think about us to cook one of your dishes with reference to you? But not only cook! We want to organise a Skype-connection with you live in our studio! Another way is you can record a short video on your cell-phone with such word like "Hello ... I'm Lorraine Pascale ... here's my kitchen ... this is where I make here ... highly recommend this dish ..." and showing your kitchen. That would be great! And our viewers would go crazy with happiness, for sure! :)'

Back home in Britain, reviewers were still musing over Lorraine's appeal. On 25 August 2012, trade publication *The Grocer* ran an article under the headline 'Lorraine Pascale blends style and substance'. Reviewer Liz Hamson wrote: 'Lorraine Pascale is a bit of a Marmite character. People either think she swans around looking pretty, making overly simple food (that as a former model she probably doesn't eat), or that she's an inventive yet practical cook who just happens to look as good as her dishes. I oscillate between the two camps but for all the superfluous shots of Pascale wandering around in fab outfits, I think she does exactly what she says on the tin; makes fast, fresh and easy food that the average (aka lazy) cook will not only want to eat, but will easily be able to cook...'

It was only natural that Lorraine's TV shows would prompt both journalists and amateur cooks to try out her recipes to see if they really were as fast, fresh and easy as she claimed. Those happy family culinary enthusiasts who couldn't make it into national print once again used YouTube to show off. One father filmed 'teenagers Carrie and Amy' creating what appeared to be a massively complicated dinner, starting with bacon and mature Cheddar twists and caramelised spiced nuts and ending with chocolate digestive cheesecake. 'Nothing went wrong,' said the girls rather too smugly after the family dining experience.

'My two-year-old son is Lorraine Pascale's biggest fan. He reads her new recipe book at bedtime and watches her TV show. Here he is making Lorraine's lamb dish – "James, do you love Lorraine.....?"'

A pair of hands was seen being washed before getting to work in 'How to make the BEST flapjacks' with the words 'sorry about rubbish picture' flashed up on the screen. The flapjacks appeared to have been successfully made.

Schoolgirls 'Beth' and 'Dixie' made blueberry and lemon cream millefeuille in just over nine minutes. 'Well, I am just so surprised we managed to pull off such a wonderful dessert and I can't wait to show it off to our friends and family...'

It seems that Lorraine has captured the cooking imagination of children as well as adults, something she truly delights in. There are several other short films posed on YouTube showing young cooks in action. And children, as we know, like to ask questions. Six-year-old Mabel posed one question in particular to Lorraine via the 'Ask a Grown-up' section of the *Guardian* in February 2013 – 'Why is cake so yummy?' Lorraine answered in full: 'Cake is so yummy because of all the stuff that goes into the bowl. You mix the butter and sugar first, then you add the eggs one by one, mix and slide everything around in the bowl, stir in the flour, and finally it starts to look like the cake mix that we know and love. I can't recommend eating the cake mix, because it does have raw eggs in it, but, secretly, licking the spoon is the best bit for me. At this point, I add chocolate, which is the naughtiest ingredient of all, but it's also what makes a cake very special. My favourite cake is a Choccy Woccy Vicky Sponge, a twist on the classic Victoria sponge. I make a chocolate sponge cake, then I soak it in sugar syrup so that it's really moist. Then I fill it with chocolate butter cream and a little strawberry jam. If I'm feeling really naughty, I spread chocolate butter icing all over the outside of the cake as well. That is obviously extra naughtiness and only for very special occasions.'

Lorraine has admitted that when she first embarked on the perilous course that is being a celebrity chef any negative criticism stung. She was, she has said, 'too overly concerned' about what others might think of her but 'now I just do my thing, smile and let the negative stuff from other people wash over me, rather than getting upset by it. It is hard sometimes but I try!' There will always be those quick to find fault but now, with her third TV series under her belt, Lorraine still had her fans, who continued to praise both her programmes and her books long after their appearance:

> 'Great cook, great looks and quite seriously well grounded. What's not to like? Go, Lorraine!'

> 'Love watching your programme, Lorraine. Don't listen to the inevitable barrage of childish comments from jealous and stuck up readers.'

> '...everything I've tried of hers has turned out brilliant... she's successful because she teaches people how to do seemingly complicated things and encourages them to try it for themselves. This nation of fast food and ready meals needs someone like her...'

Christmas came early for Lorraine that year – well, with a bit of TV licence it did. She was back on *Saturday Kitchen* on 22 October 2012 in a Christmas 'special'. This saw Lorraine getting into the festive spirit with a background of tree and decorations and wearing a bright-red patterned sweater (she was supporting a Save the Children fund-raiser that urges people to wear a 'bright festive knit' and donate £1 to the charity) before it was 'time to stuff the bird'. She prepared and cooked a turkey accompanied by alcoholic gravy. Then a full Christmas dinner was served to family and friends. If this was shown in October, one wonders just when it was recorded and whether Lorraine's mum and dad and assorted guests sat down to the festive feast in summer.

Much closer to the real day was a repeat in December of *Lorraine's Last Minute Christmas* from the previous year – 'I watched Lorraine Pascale make these rather special star mince pies on her *Last Minute Christmas* show last year. These are perfect for entertainment and are ready in a jiffy. The job will be even quicker if you buy sheets of ready-rolled puff pastry (which I did). I'm planning on making plenty of batches of these this year... enjoy!'

Lorraine had certainly become a celebrity in her own right now, with invitations to glittering events arriving on a regular basis. Thus, she was photographed attending the Sky Women in Film and Television Awards at London's Hilton Hotel in November due to her TV connections, and a week later, at The Prince's Trust Comedy Gala at the Royal Albert Hall in her capacity as an ambassador of the Trust.

At the end of 2012, her books were still selling well, although Jamie Oliver was at the number one position with his *Jamie's 15-Minute Meals* – his third consecutive Christmas bestseller. Lorraine was still well in the top 100, however, at No. 35 – and above Nigella Lawson. But sites aimed at the relevant section of the population made the point: 'The bestselling black author of 2012 is Lorraine Pascale for her TV tie-in book *Fast, Fresh and Easy Food*. That is 174,654 copies of real books sold at bookshops – in only 5 months, as it was published in August. That is good news. She's fabulous, her food is good and the recipes work.'

As has already been noted, when a chef bravely puts a foot in the amphitheatre that is television, not all spectators will applaud. And so it was at the conclusion of a year that had seen three bestselling books and three series with high viewing figures – and with Turkey being the latest country to take her *Home Cooking Made Easy* series – Lorraine faced a bit of a backlash. But she wasn't alone in this particular criticism of her food not being as healthy as it could be. Fellow TV chefs Jamie Oliver and Nigella Lawson – both known to demonstrate high passion when it comes to creative culinary skills on camera – were also in the firing line. It was in December 2012 that the results of research carried out by the NHS Tees and Newcastle University were published. The two groups had tested and analysed both superchef cooking and supermarket meals in a quest to find out which was healthier (in Lorraine's case they used recipes from her *Baking Made Easy* book – it might perhaps have been a bit fairer had they waited for *Fast, Fresh and Easy Food*, the recipe book in which Lorraine emphasised her preference for fresh food). Anyway, their verdict was not good:

'Upon analysis, researchers discovered that recipes by TV chefs were less healthy than ready meals, comprising of significantly more energy, protein, fat and saturated fat, and a lower total of fibre per portion than the ready meals.' If this wasn't damaging enough, it was also determined that the recipes from the TV chefs were more likely to achieve 'red traffic light' labels according to the Food Standards Agency criteria than ready meals. For those unaware, the traffic light system works by having a postage-stamp sized sticker that states the percentage of a person's recommended daily allowance contained in each product – red for high, amber for medium and green for low.'

There was further bad news for the disciples of supercooks – only slightly softened by the fact that readymade meals did not fare so well either:

'It was calculated that on average, the recipes conjured up by the celebrity chefs contained 2,530 calories per portion and the ready meals fared slightly better, with 2,067 per portion. However, it was found that no meal option from either group reached the criteria set by the World Health Organisation for a "balanced healthy meal". In addition, the study authors stress that any salt used for seasoning was not considered in their analysis. This study shows that neither recipes created by popular television chefs nor ready meals produced by three leading UK supermarket chains meet national or international nutritional standards for a balanced diet. The recipes seemed to be less healthy than the ready meals on several metrics.'

Strangely, the report seemed to imply that despite Lorraine's dashing around the world to seek out all sorts of fresh ingredients – and similar determination by her fellow TV chefs to source good stuff – none of them came up to scratch:

'Good nutritional intake is likely to be derived from home cooking of nutritionally balanced recipes primarily using raw ingredients, rather than relying on ready meals or recipes by television chefs.'

But there was support of Lorraine and other TV chefs from certain quarters too. Writing in the *Standard*, Richard Godwin was not convinced by the results of the survey. 'Actually, the study is a pretty high-cholesterol example of how "science" in pursuit of an easy headline sends out completely the wrong message. The reason that obesity has overtaken malnutrition is not because people are trying to copy Lorraine Pascale. It is because they are eating crap. That is the main problem. Anything that connects taste to effort and knowledge, rather than the instant gratification offered by our industrialised food processes, spreads a deeper long-term benefit.'

It was only natural – well, as natural as their nemesis deemed them to be – that the TV cooks should hit back. A spokesperson for Lorraine gave a fair enough response: 'Some of the recipes in Lorraine's book are healthy, some not quite so much so. There are plenty of salads, soups and light meals as well as the richer dishes. Her books and shows to date haven't been about healthy eating; they are about cooking – and Lorraine has confessed to her most-used ingredients being Marsala (a Sicilian wine), salt and butter.'

Lorraine herself poses a good question when it comes to the whole healthy eating and obesity debate: 'I'm not sure how accurate the Government advice on healthy eating is. The pyramid system urges us to eat lots of bread and potatoes. That advice started in the Eighties. That's when the obesity epidemic began. The question is, if the Government's advice is right, why are we as a nation getting bigger?'

Maybe the timing wasn't perfect, but in the following January, Lorraine did an economy food 'taste test' for the *Observer* in which she sampled and rated 'essentials from tinned soup to sausages' (and also baked beans, cheese and strawberry jam) from supermarkets Waitrose, Tesco, Morrisons and the Co-operative. The article opened up quite a big forum debate with most commentators pouring scorn on supermarket 'basics'. 'So why is this chef and the *Observer* even considering doing this sort of thing? It doesn't matter how many stars that you give crap, it's still crap. Fill your meals with this "value" stuff and you will end up obese. A more instructive thing to do would be to put the nutritional info next to each product in your test. Eat fresh food from local producers and local shops, you might eat less but you'll feel better.'

'Personal tastes will vary but good to see Ms Pascale doesn't mind getting her er... hands dirty reviewing economy products,' noted another.

Voicing her opinion about a subject she no doubt felt more at home with, the next month Lorraine elaborated on her strong feelings over child obesity. She was answering a report that called for cookery lessons to go on the school curriculum along with the more traditional subjects of English and maths. It was a subject close to Lorraine's heart for she knew just how useful such lessons could be, having enjoyed them so much when she was at school. Writing in the *Sun*, she said: 'It's mad we don't teach kids basic life skills. At school they learn maths, geography, science... all geared towards passing exams. But often they don't learn how to cook or what foods are good for them. Successive governments have had their heads in the sand over childhood obesity. Now it's an epidemic. Kids today have a shorter life expectancy than their parents – and that's down to poor diet. Not every school has the facilities to offer practical cookery classes but they can all teach the theory. MPs, as always, will moan about cost. But obesity already costs the NHS £5.1BILLION a year. And 30 per cent of kids aged 2 to 15 are now obese.'

Lorraine referred to fellow TV chef Jamie Oliver's healthy school dinners campaign from a few years before, describing it as 'brilliant', but added that it was time to take good eating to 'the next step'. If she were in charge, she would 'make fruit and veg as crucial a part of school life as reading and writing. I'd show kids how fruit and veg can help them learn better and run faster. I had monthly cookery lessons at school, with the kids bringing in their own ingredients. As well as developing a life skill, we also got better with numbers and learnt how to share. Above all, cooking is fun. It's hands-on and messy. And you get to eat what you just made.'

Lorraine said it was 'scary' that teenagers leave school without knowing 'how to boil an egg' and advocated the teaching of ten simple dishes as a basis to cooking skills. She added: 'And it's not enough to educate children. We need to coach parents too.

Eating well on a budget is a challenge – which is why the Government must help. If we cut down the amount of processed food we eat, we can turn this epidemic around. I believe passionately in this cause. After all, you are what you eat.'

All in all, Lorraine gave an excellent account for herself, fending off any criticism that she had had over her lack of concern for healthy food prepared on her TV programmes and highlighting the whole problem of the nation's obesity. She had become a pretty good ambassador for both causes.

Chapter 11

Racist rants

It was in 2011 that Lorraine first became victim to a series of vicious 'tweets'. One, sent on 12 November, was particularly obnoxious and racist: 'Don't really need you telling us how to forcefeed kids you f***** dumb n*****. Get off the TV c*** and know your place.' An earlier message had called her an 'ugly, unevolved animal'. They were two in a series sent over several months by the American-based writer and which came through the account @spiderman. This was just one of the aliases used to abuse Lorraine. Her tormentor re-opened accounts each time he was shut down though Lorraine continually blocked and reported him. Although British Twitter intervened, it was a problem emanating from America with the site's managers seemingly doing little to halt the very public and vilifying comments. Lorraine's ordeal was made even worse by the reaction of some equally racist observers of her plight: 'When I saw this I couldn't stop laughing. I hate this woman; she's one of them people who because she was raised by a white family thinks racism doesn't exist. I'm glad this has happened to her.'

Meanwhile, Lorraine's popularity still necessitated an official site to keep fans informed of her latest ventures. And in August 2012 web design company Ten4 updated her authorised site, commissioned by Lorraine's management company, James Grant. Launching the site, the company said its brief was to create a 'bright and clean online presence' not only to promote her latest book *Fast, Fresh and Easy Food*, but also to 'showcase' recipes from her books and provide followers with a picture gallery, videos, news and biography.

Exactly a year later, Lorraine's tormentor started again. Even with the prejudice she had experienced in her earlier years, naturally she found these particular rants horrifying, unwarranted and unacceptable. She thought long and hard about how to react before deciding to expose the writer for the anonymous and malicious coward he was. And so she copied the words and posted them on her Twitter page, together with the author's 'tag'. Lorraine added her own comments: 'Unpleasant tweet to get this morning coming right up. A very sad state of affairs.' She then reported the racist message to London's Metropolitan Police. Meanwhile, she asked her 51,000 followers on Twitter: 'How is it that someone in the US is free to send me vile racist tweets on a daily basis yet Twitter does nothing to stop him? I can't keep quiet any longer. It hurts...' The loathsome taunts came at the rate of up to 25 tweets a week with her tormentor alternating between bombarding her every day to then going quiet for a few days. It was, she said, 'systematic abuse' and even though she had grown up with racist ignorance, this was the worst she had ever experienced and was 'horrific'.

Fellow tweeters, disgusted by her ordeal, rushed to comfort and support Lorraine. 'You are absolute scum,' said one about her tormentor. 'You shouldn't talk to Lorraine or anyone like that. Talent earns its place at the table.' Another wrote: 'Hope you get what is coming to you.' It was no consolation to Lorraine that the ranter had posted racist tweets about others on his public page, including American President Barack Obama. She said: 'I am hurt, shocked and saddened by the comments this person has made against me. Sadly this is not the first time racist comments have been directed at me on Twitter. I have therefore decided to report it to the police and speak out. I do this for myself and countless others who have to deal with this kind of abuse on a daily basis and are powerless to stop it.'

Lorraine praised British Twitter for acting on her complaints but was frustrated by the American side not doing enough to stop the internet troll abuse. The user later had his account suspended yet again but there were fears he would strike again. Said Lorraine: 'I'm not looking for sympathy. I just think that if it's happening to me it is almost certainly happening to others who are even less able to do anything about it.'

That same month, November 2012, Lorraine used her Twitter pages to voice her feelings on the general issue of racial prejudice. On 30 November, referring to the British Nationalist Party coming third in the local elections in Rotherham, she wrote: 'Post Rotherham by-election results. Just reading the BNP policy on immigration. Stunned.

'Still, if they ever did get their way, it looks like there is a free ticket for me back to the Caribbean in the offing!'

Sadly taunts via the internet are not the only verbal racist attacks Lorraine experiences. She has told how at least once a month someone will shout at her in the street. Of course nothing can justify such abuse but it is something she has learned to live with as a black female chef with a high public profile. She has to ask herself whether to continually take it to heart or deal with it. It hurts her deeply but she has said she has learned to brush it off, even though she is ever conscious of her colour. Lorraine once tweeted from a restaurant in Chelsea to say she felt 'very out of place... am most definitely the only, shall we say, non-blonde in the village'. And with the same hint of discomfort she also commented on how she had watched a television show in America in which a family heads out West for home schooling and pioneer cooking, adding: 'It was very white, the area, in the middle of nowhere. I wouldn't have been all that welcome.'

In December 2012, she told how a landlord of a country pub muttered racist comments suggesting that all 'n****rs' should 'go home' but then offered to serve her because his wife was a fan of her cookery programme. Said Lorraine: 'I looked at him with my best bitchy LP stare, paid for my pork scratchings and walked right out of that pub...' It was yet another occasion when she simply had to bite her tongue and move on. 'When these things happen I have to decide if I am going to let it get to me or not. It's just about seeing the funny side of it. Laugh it off and feel sorry for them.'

The unpleasant encounter was reported widely in the national press and prompted comment on the *Daily Mail*'s online site:

'Lorraine is simply stunning, a truly beautiful

woman. As for the pub landlord he clearly has the IQ of a squashed slug and that's being generous.'

'She is so beautiful. What a fool this person is.'

'Why are some certain people mentioning "political correctness"? What does this have to do with that? So in your eyes it's ok for this man to call Lorraine a n***** and tell her to leave based on the fact she's black? I'm sure you people wouldn't be mentioning political correctness if it was a black man calling Jamie Oliver a h*****. Racism is pure wrong and I'm glad the majority of comments recognise that.'

There was naturally the odd offensive remark by lesser mortals.

Lorraine's appearance on Facebook is not without its unsavoury contributors either. That same month 'Phill Rocker' – 'freelance photographer' and 'porn model' – posed two questions: 'Hi Lorraine. Do you want to have sex?' and 'Can I make love to you making Pavlova...?' Happily, most of her 35,000 or so Facebook followers (she joined in February 2011) are decent human beings. But could it get any worse? The Twitter incidents were all reported in the press at the time but there was to be yet another episode which did not become widely public. For Lorraine was not to escape abusive taunts even at Christmas that year when time with her family was blighted by the worst and most disgusting racist tweets from the post of dog @vanskkkuller: 'How was X-mass at the London Zoo with your BLACK MONKEY family. Did you all smear yourself in SHIT and drink eggnog?' and 'Go back to the London Zoo you BLACK MONKEY!'

They were enough to provoke the support of black MP Diane Abbott, who urged Lorraine to 'Ignore. Ignore. Ignore. A response is what he wants.' Lorraine was philosophical: 'Very tedious tweets devoid of Chrissy spirit.' And despite what her MP friend had advised, Lorraine tweeted back: 'Racism is so 1970s. Get with the programme? Have you nothing better to do. You really are tedious to the extreme. Yawn. Yawn.' She reassured her Twitter followers that she was 'totally fine' but frustrated at her battle to make it stop, adding, 'Twitter is a great platform so let's now just focus on the good stuff.' One follower tweeted to say she had reported the abuse from 'the creature'. Others commiserated with Lorraine for 'having, once more, to read such comments'.

It might seem that Lorraine only uses the social media Twitter site – on which she describes herself as 'foodie chick, flavour lover, traveller, gym bunny, avid telly watcher' and 'reader of inspirational book stuff' – to express strong feelings against criticism, prejudice and her personal views on adoption issues. That isn't so, even if she once commented: 'Dulux-style-skin colour matching of children to parents is not the primary route to a successful placement...' In fact, she is a self-confessed addictive tweeter, regularly updating fellow tweeters on her day-to-day doings and thoughts. Some are trivial musings:

'Anyone else braving the shops today? I'm off to buy pork shoulder, mascara and a Christmas tree. A little something for everyone...!' 9 December 2012

'At the desk early today writing recipes and watching London slowly awake.' 9 December 2012.

'Just watching *EastEnders*... very weird to hear my name announced at the end of it saying that the show was on.... freaky!' 17 September 2012.

But other tweets give an insight into Lorraine's hectic life, the pressures it brings (including working until the early hours) and how she is still occasionally blighted by the depression that has always haunted her:

'Monday Morning blues... got the mountainous week ahead to navigate. Very much pining for Sunday's hazy lazyness and big hearty roasts.' 9 December 2012.

'I'm just not sure that writing a recipe for pear, chocolate and almond Christmas cake at silly o'clock is really all that necessary.' 28 November 2012.

'Can't sleep so furiously writing down some new recipe inspiration. Awake at 1am on a school night. Not impressive. Not very impressive at all.' 28 November 2012.

'In a melancholic mood so must indulge in the therapy of baking. Wholewheat bread with toasted pecans.' 26 November 2012.

'Just woke up post my 4am recipe writing spree with my laptop stuck to my cheek. Now have an apple shaped dent on my face.' 23 November 2012.

'Strangely awake at this unsociable hour and struck with a flurry of recipe inspiration. It's just me and my tea and my blue laptop light.' 22 November 2012.

And naturally, there are copious references to food:

'Stuffed with Mulligatawny, lamb, Brussels sprouts, butternut squash and a whole host of other lovelies. My goodness, I do love a Sunday.' 9 December 2012.

'Lamb roasting in the oven and caramelized butternut squash, shredded sprouts, rosemary and red onions... house smelling gawgeous.' 9 December 2012.

'Just cooked a mighty fine steamed pudding with chocolate, pear and stem ginger... oh my goodness... That was proper tasty.' 8 December 2012.

'Six hours of steaming and the Christmas pudding is finally cooked. Christmas pudding, do you make yours from scratch or buy it?' 3 December 2012.

'Recipe testing a Christmas lunch today. Turkey is in the oven, spuds have just gone in, sprouts, stuffing, carrots on standby... Oh yes.' 25 November 2012.

'The cake morphed into bread (no eggs) & so a honey& toasted walnut loaf is now baking in the oven. Bready smells meandering around the house.' 25 September 2012.

'Slow roast lamb with Aussie Chardonnay, rosemary, sage and bay is roasting away in the oven smelling pure blissfulness. 90 mins to go.' 23 September 2012.

Lorraine also uses this forum not only to ask questions – 'Does anyone know the average weekly spend on groceries for a UK family of four please?' – and answer those relating to cookery quandaries and to keep fans posted on her news, but she often asks for advice on what to wear (with an accompanying posted photograph), to pass on lifestyle snippets and to re-tweet information she feels is of interest. She also asks for help with recipe ideas and keeps her Twitter friends up to date when writing her books: 'Writing a load of recipes and struggling not to put an exclamation mark on the end of every sentence. Must be too much time on Twitter.' All, of course, keep her followers enthralled.

But one piece of information she omitted in December 2012 was that with model agency Storm's boss Sarah Doukas and Lorraine sharing 'the same attitude' about business – a remark made in the 2010 *Red* Magazine interview – she had also now signed up with Models 1 in its 'special bookings' section. This presented Lorraine with the opportunity for photo shoots which weren't always strictly glamour fashion ones.

Her decision was undoubtedly backed by Doukas, of whom Lorraine once said: 'She always wants me to think bigger.'

Chapter 12

Dealing with demons

Through the bad times, it is Lorraine's close circle of friends who have kept her going and been there for her. She has said she has spent a lot of time talking to them about her earlier years. This has been much more cathartic than talking to any social worker. Lorraine places a lot of importance on those who are privileged to earn her trust. She has praised her management company for looking after her when she was 'lying in a provincial heap on the floor', her model agency for its maternal concern and those good friends and family members who have seen her through good times and bad.

But there has also been support from professionals

from whom Lorraine has attempted to seek understanding of her often dismal younger days. Sessions of therapy have helped her to deal with the emotional scars of her early life – what she describes as a 'ruptured childhood'. She has never been in denial about what has happened to her but there will always be ghosts that need to be laid to rest. Lorraine still has therapy to keep her balanced about the past but one wonders if she will completely recover. She says: 'It's worked but it's taken me time. In my twenties I was very angry about all the rejection and what had happened. There was a lot of "why me, why did you do it?" to my mum. And I spent a lot of my thirties trying to work out what I wanted to do with my life. Even my counsellor says, "Why are you not a basket case?" For a while I probably was.'

'I'm looking forward to my forties because I think I'm in a good place but when something awful happens you have to grieve it, let it out. The worst thing you can do is push it down. Things affect us in different ways. I've met people whose father left home for six months and it damaged them for life.'

Lorraine has admitted to suffering from depression and there are occasions – her 'duvet days' – when she takes to her bed and immerses herself in a good book to settle her mind: 'A duvet day is fine. I read. I love quotes.' She has also said that making bread acts as a kind of therapy for her – 'it gets me out of my black dog blues'. There are still the ever-present memories that prey on her, though. 'Other people go through terrible things, they get tortured for instance, and they seem to cope. I'm quite resilient but I've done a lot of work on myself. It probably was traumatic but I've always had a real British stiff upper lip and thought you just have to get on with it. There's always someone with a worse story and some with better ones. In a way I think it's been good for me – it's taught me to have drive.'

This drive sees Lorraine determined to maintain support of children's charities despite her hectic life. In May 2012 she gave her public support to Foster Care Fortnight. 'I have such admiration for those that foster and indeed take the steps toward fostering a child. There are so many incredible people out there who would make – and make – incredible foster carers, and there are also many children out there who need those very people to be foster carers to them.' She also wrote a poignant, very personal account of her own experiences to highlight Foster Care Fortnight on its website. It highlights just how eager she was for the happy, warm environment of family life:

'I first went into care when I was eight years old. It was a frightening experience, leaving home. Luckily the social workers had managed to find me a family who were in the same town where I grew up and I kind of already knew one of the girls in the family, who had also been adopted.

'What struck me when I first entered the house was this warm buzz of chaos. Children playing around everywhere, toys scattered over the floor, the upbeat noise of a children's TV show on in the background. And then I met my foster carer. She had a huge smile, big brown friendly eyes, a mass of curly hair and a hug like a big warm duvet. I met all of the other children (they had several fostered/adopted children there) and then we all sat around the table and ate some food.

'They were so lovely and did not ask me lots and lots of questions. They just went about their business talking to each other about their day and what they were going to do tomorrow. And every so often the lady carer would give me the most comforting soft smile.

'So it was really from the very beginning that I felt at home there. It was clearly a very happy household with very happy children and a couple who loved each other very much. And because of that, in time, I felt happy and safe. I can only speak for myself but it is very hard to feel safe in foster care. That is the word which always rang in my ears. Safe. I just wanted to feel safe and secure, but being in care (even at the age of eight), I knew that this was only going to be a temporary stop. I knew that sooner or later, it would be time to pack the bags and go. But for what I needed at that time, which was love, support, and a "constant" in my life and knowing that there was a hot meal on the table when I came home and always a big hug on standby, it was enough.

'On the weekends, one of the older children there would pretend to be teacher and give all the younger children fun lessons in English and other subjects. Those were such pleasurable times, just sitting there with everyone, laughing and joking and feeling part of a big contented family with such a welcoming and compassionate heart.

'I can imagine at times I must have been quite challenging, like most children are at different times, but having a family who were calm and knew themselves and their own foibles well, along with the ability to know how to talk to me and how to regulate the many different emotions which often come with a child who has been in care was an incredibly precious gift to me.

'They just loved, listened, hugged, were patient, compassionate, did not judge and were always there.'

It was at this foster home, too where Lorraine's love of cooking was encouraged – 'It inspired me,' she said.

Lorraine has also said that 'knowing that in the end

everything would be OK' is what kept her strong during her foster care years. In an interview with *Who Cares?* magazine she gave her personal advice to children in care: 'Stay strong, find someone to talk to. Cry when you need to. Above all, know that it is not your fault that you are in care. Sometimes life gives us something that we are not expecting. Tell yourself that you are loveable and that if there are bad times they will pass. The bad days always pass.' If there was anything good about her early days in care, Lorraine has said it was 'meeting new people' – a somewhat ambiguous statement considering the trauma the little girl must have experienced each time new faces entered her life.

And when it comes to the colour of skin in regard to adoption her belief is simply expressed: 'How can ethnicity be more important than love?'

As well as being involved in TACT, Lorraine supports other charities too. In May 2011, she fronted 'Wake up Your Mind' to raise money for the mental health charity Mind. The campaign was aimed at improving mental health at work and supporters were asked to hold breakfasts on 20 May 'to improve morale'. Lorraine's contribution was a flapjack recipe: 'An energy-packed breakfast is an essential way to start the working day and my flapjacks are the perfect occasional treat to enjoy with colleagues while raising funds for Mind.'

In 2012 Lorraine became an ambassador for Rays of Sunshine, a charity set up in 2004 to make wishes come true for terminally and seriously ill children between the ages of 3–18 in the United Kingdom. It also helps to buy equipment for hospitals, hospices and specialist schools. Lorraine first came into contact with the charity in 2011 when she took time out from her manic schedule to fulfil a wish for a young girl suffering from Acute Lymphoblastic Leukaemia. Benita, aged nine, had expressed her ambition be a chef when she grew up and her greatest wish was to cook with Lorraine, who visited her at her London home to spend the afternoon cooking Benita's favourite dishes. Said Lorraine: 'I am delighted to take on the role of ambassador for Rays of Sunshine. Spending time with Benita and her family last year gave me first-hand experience of the difference a wish can make. I look forward to helping out whenever I can.' Jane Sharpe, CEO of Rays of Sunshine, added: 'We are absolutely thrilled that Lorraine has agreed to become our newest ambassador. As well as being a huge talent, Lorraine is a down-to-earth mum with a natural compassion. Her support will help us to brighten up the lives of some of the UK's most deserving children.'

In October 2012 Lorraine donated another of her recipes and wrote the foreword for the charity's celebrity cookbook, *A Dish For A Wish*. She said:

'I hope the book will brighten up your kitchen, as every copy sold will help to brighten up the life of a seriously ill child in the UK.' (Lorraine's continued support came by way of donating one of her recipes – cookies and cream fudge brownies – to 'Bake a Wish' for the charity's 'Have a Heart' appeal. She said: 'Chocolate brownies have been a favourite of mine since I was eight years old and I'm sure they will be a big hit and raise lots of cash.')

It was a particularly busy month for Lorraine. On 6 October she helped out at the Million Meal Appeal in her capacity as ambassador for FareShare, an organisation that supplies food to the vulnerable and needy. The collection was held at the Sainsbury's store in London's Cromwell Road, with Sainsbury's matching each meal donated. Whether it was the Lorraine connection that drew huge support or just magnanimous supporters, but around two million meals were donated. Said Lorraine: 'The response has been amazing. We've raised millions of meals, one extra item at a time. It really shows how little actions can make a huge difference if we work together.'

Lorraine made an appearance on ITV's *This Morning* on 21 October (she cooked her tarragon pork chops with a little help from presenters Eamonn Holmes and Ruth Langsford but confessed she was a 'pizza and chips kid') before flying off to Ghana to film for a series highlighting support given by Comic

Relief. So keen was she to go that when initially approached about the visit, Lorraine said: 'I already had my suitcase mentally packed.' Her reports featured in the *Great Comic Relief Bake Off*, involving 16 TV personalities, which was shown on four consecutive nights the following January. Lorraine reported on projects that had blossomed through Comic Relief funding: the Grace School, which provides vulnerable children with an education, a cocoa co-operative and Tree Aid, which gives villagers the opportunity to harvest honey in the dry season.

The plight of some of the country's street children touched Lorraine the most. She later told of a visit to a lorry park on the outskirts of town where children who had run away from home earned money carrying goods for the lorry drivers or selling water. At night, the children huddle together and sleep on the pavements. Lorraine described the 'uncomfortable atmosphere' and how she felt threatened by men who were either drunk or on drugs. Some of the children now have a night shelter to go to, however Lorraine said: 'As a mum I hate to think of these youngsters being in such a vulnerable situation. This is no place for children, but thank goodness there is an alternative.'

It was in the first episode when Lorraine was seen visiting Accra when she came across one particular project close to her heart. She spent time with the employees of the Virtuous Woman's Bakery, which employs women who would otherwise be struggling to support their children. Lorraine was delighted to see that on the day of her visit, the women were baking bread. As usual, she sent regular tweets about her activities:

'I have left half of the family at home and I'm off to Ghana with Comic Relief to see some of the foodie Comic Relief Projects :-)'

'Some amazing projects out here. Comic Relief doing incredible work. Missing London, family, friends and Smarticus a little bit though :-)x.' [Smarticus is the name Lorraine has given to her Smart Car.]

'Day 4; Ghana log. Sitting with the crew in middle of nowhere drinking ice-cold beers under a tree, loud crickets and a bright white moon.'

'Last night in Ghana. Can't wait to see the rest of the family when I get home :-)'

Lorraine returned home on 26 October, tweeting: 'So lovely to be back in London after an intrepid trip to Northern Ghana with Comic Relief. Looking forward to a hot cup of tea and a sit down.'

The whole visit was to have a lasting effect on her.

'When I was modelling I went to Africa on photo shoots but nothing could have prepared me for the intensity of the poverty in Ghana.'

That same month Lorraine was announced as a nominee for the Favourite Female TV Star at the eighth Screen Nation Film and Television Awards – 'Europe's only international celebration of black achievement in film and television.' Lorraine – nominated for *Fast, Fresh and Easy Food* – was in a list that included singer Alesha Dixon and actresses Angela Griffiths and Chelsee Healey. The awards ceremony – hailed the 'Black Baftas' – was scheduled to take place at London's Park Plaza Hotel on 11 November but was mysteriously cancelled two days before. Behind-the-scenes problems were blamed and there was criticism over a report in the *Guardian* under the headline 'Do Black Actors Still Need the Screen Nation Awards?' This was a particularly sensitive issue as the event also marked the 50th Independence anniversaries of Jamaica and Trinidad and Tobago. The ceremony eventually went ahead on 17 February 2013. Sadly for Lorraine she did not win her category, with the award going to *EastEnders* actress Tameka Empson.

Finding her feet, regaining confidence and going on to prove herself, Lorraine has now found her niche through a combination of hard work and determination. Her efforts won praise from one commentator. On the In-SpireLS site she was hailed as a woman who had made it in business without a man: 'In the modern age we live in, women have elevated themselves through sheer determination, hard graft and even in court, to gain equality in a lot of areas such as pay, electoral responsibility and rights; this is all rightly so. Women own companies, they manage football clubs, they inspire, they effect change. A lot's changed. Lorraine Pascale the accomplished baker started her career as a model and was the first British black model to front the USA edition of *Elle*. Following this she trained to be a mechanic. And why shouldn't she? It's unlikely that she sits at home with a plug, thinking, "I wish there was a man here to wire this for me!" No, she doesn't – she'll do it. Women neither like to be nor need to be dependent on a man.'

Chapter 13

Recipe for happiness

After her traumatic early life, Lorraine has said that she feels positive about the future. Having reached her landmark birthday she is now looking forward to being a successful woman in her forties. She feels she is in 'a good place'. That term could apply literally to the personal and emotional calm she mostly possesses nowadays, as well as to the times when she is at her most happy and contented – in her favourite room mixing, mashing and making good food with the television on in the background. She is, she has said, sometimes like a 'mad scientist' who seeks different ways to make a dish 'sexier' and who is still amazed at the 'magical transition' of a baked dish emerging from the oven. And all the while, Lorraine maintains passion in her cooking. 'Looking back at my life, with its inevitable highs and lows, I now realise that I have always found a sense of purpose and strength of mind when I am in the kitchen. The phone will ring and all the dramas will rage outside, but cooking is where I find my peace and quiet. I believe this is called being "in flow" – when you are so passionately and happily engaged in an activity that you lose all track of time.'

Lorraine's cooking karma carries on outside where she has turned the terrace of her flat into a miniature garden, where she grows herbs, tomatoes, red peppers and chillies – all fresh ingredients to be used in her cooking. She admits she is not always brilliant at cultivating what is growing in her little pots and often calls on the help of her dad, who makes the trip from his Surrey home to give a hand (his pear trees also give Lorraine a good supply for her recipes). Having someone around to tend the healthy stuff is probably more than helpful, with Lorraine admitting she is facing a 'mini mid-life crisis' and trying to beat the temptation of not-so-healthy food. Fruit and vegetables therefore regularly feature on the plates of the Pascale household.

In her organised way, each Sunday, with glass of wine in hand, Lorraine will go online to shop for five days' worth of meals. If it all goes awry, she has no qualms about being 'caught red-handed' in a supermarket buying ready-made food – or ordering a pizza. But there is no question of Lorraine's association between lovingly made food and the comfort it can bring. She was asked by adoption magazine *Family Matters* what two-course meal she would prepare to welcome home an adopted child and came up with slow roast leg of lamb, followed by little, warm Bramley apple pies. Comfort indeed.

Still very close to all her family – especially her brother Jason, who works as an assistant producer for IMG Media (though she only really 'talks' to half-sister Francesca on Facebook) – Lorraine is even considering adopting a child if the right time comes because 'I think it's a wonderful thing to do.' Having had such painful personal experience – she is still afraid of the dark – it is not something she would enter into lightly, though. She has also come to the point of trust with her partner Doherty that means she 'would possibly' like to get married again. But ever cautious, she describes her long-term plans as 'all maybes and possibilities at the moment'. There could even be the opening of a Lorraine Pascale restaurant.

On the fame front, Lorraine still finds it incredible that she is recognised by those in the same business – once being taken aback to be approached by Heston Blumenthal while lunching at his Diner restaurant. 'He said hello and we had a chat, which was lovely,' she said. 'Heston Blumenthal is a genius. I wasn't expecting him to know who I was, but he did.' Fame often means you get other television offers, of course but although now well at ease on TV, Lorraine knows her limits. Despite being asked, she has turned down *Strictly Come Dancing* – although a Digital Spy website announcement in December 2012 announced she was in the line-up for the next series, alongside Leona Lewis, Vanessa Feltz and Chris Tarrant – and *Dancing on Ice*. She's just too clumsy, she says, and the idea of embarrassing herself out of her comfort zone is just too much.

At the end of 2012 Lorraine was already working on recipes for her fourth cookery book – and wondering what to call it. 'Would you prefer to buy a book which said "skinny food" or "healthier food"... all tasty and yummy still,' she tweeted at one point. She was also researching the weekly cost of feeding a family of four and casting around friends, fans and followers for their ideas while busy in the kitchen testing her new dishes. There were hints that she would include lots of puddings and desserts in her new book, titled *A Lighter Way to Bake*.

Lorraine also teamed up with the Duchess of Cambridge to plan a Valentine's Day meal for Prince Charles. The aim was to have something special for The Prince's Trust Ball in 2013. In her typical enthusiasm she declared that she was 'flooded' with ideas and that it was all 'very exciting'. She was in charge of creating petits fours and the main dish, and she and her Royal collaborator did tasting sessions together. This was not Lorraine's first involvement with a right Royal banquet for she and other celebrities had linked up with Save the Children to suggest fund-raising ideas for the charity linked to Kate and William's wedding in April 2011. Her suggested Royal Wedding Street Party menu was canapés of Parmesan and poppy seed lollipops (the very same ones which she had shown how to make on her debut TV programme) and sun-dried and rosemary palmiers, a starter of whisky and chilli prawns, a main course of peppered beef with cognac and parma-wrapped green beans and another of her signature favourites, blueberry and lemon millefeuilles for dessert.

It had been a very sociable Christmas with Lorraine enjoying not one, but three Christmas dinners with friends and family. She had also taken some time out on Christmas Day to visit the Tope Project in London. Staffed by volunteers, the project aims at easing the loneliness for 'care-experienced young people', so one can understand why Lorraine was more than happy to give up some of her time to share its Christmas event, during which she signed books and talked about her own experiences in care. She left the event promising that she would continue to support the group in any way she could.

As 2012 came to a close, Lorraine was also preparing for an appearance at one of Fortnum & Mason's Chefs Dinners on 30 January. She was to be the chef for the night at the £50-a-head dinner and as 'the hottest home baking heroine' was also to give a demonstration, or as Fortnum's proclaimed, 'will share her expertise, her passion for innovation and her all-time favourites, both savoury and sweet.' Lorraine's menu started with her much-favoured poppy seed lollipops (again with Parmesan), followed by roasted butternut squash soup with chilli and pain d'epi (made with a strong white flour) and Rioja braised lamb shank with chorizo and garlic, a palate cleanser of limoncello jell-o shot and a dessert of mascarpone and ginger crème brûlée. Wines were chosen to accompany each course – though perhaps the choice was left to the sommelier as Lorraine has admitted that she is 'embarrassingly still stuck in the 90s' when it comes to wine and tends to stick to a 'good Aussie chardonnay' with her Sunday roast. The meal ended with Guyata coffee from Colombia.

In the run up to this event, visitors to the store were treated to a spectacular window display. A 'Lorraine Pascale' bust styled to look like Marie Antoinette – and with something of a resemblance to Lorraine – sat in the window for two weeks and proved a real show-stopper to passers-by. Perched on a white pedestal and with the lower half dressed in pink and gold, it had an impossibly high elaborate white 'wig' featuring pots, pans and other kitchen utensils, as well as edible items such as lemons. Alongside was a large bowl and plinth also displaying food and bottles. Copies of Lorraine's *Fast, Fresh and Easy Food* were strategically placed around the display.

Lorraine was also invited to join Fortnum's in-store pop-up bakery, which launched that month. And keeping up with her support of charities, she was amongst a group of celebrity chefs who supplied recipes for a tea party in aid of the National Rheumatoid Arthritis Society (NRAS) based in Maidenhead, Berkshire.

Lorraine's column in the *Sun on Sunday* was still proving popular with New Year advice on how to beat the after-Christmas blues with comfort food and ideas for unusual weekend brunches: 'On sleepy Saturday and Sunday mornings, sometimes a bowl of Shreddies or Crunchy Nut Cornflakes just isn't enough. After a good read of the papers or a lazy lie-in with a loved one, treat yourself to these brunches for something a little different. Or even better, get someone else to spoil you and leave them to make it! Just the ticket to start your day at the weekend.'

The start of 2013 also saw Lorraine maintaining her support of charities. On 15 January, Smooth Radio announced that she was amongst the celebrity chefs who had agreed to be part of the radio station's fund-raising for Macmillan Cancer Support. It was running a Chef of the Week spot and Lorraine was amongst those lined up to give listeners their tips and recipes, 'providing inspiration' for the station's Starlight Supper dinner parties which it was encouraging keen cooks across the country to host. Guests would be asked to make a donation to the charity.

On 14 February 2013, Lorraine cooked up her treat for the Invest in Futures gala dinner, a Prince's Trust Event. Her ginger panna cotta, champagne jelly and pear dessert in a swan ice sculpture was hailed 'amazing!'. That same month she linked up with American Express to inspire young adults to reach their potential in life. Reflecting on Lorraine's own life, it would be hard to find a better ambassador – 'Personal fulfilment is one of the most important things and we should never stop trying to follow our dreams. I have never stopped trying to follow my dreams.' The company had made a study of more than 2,000 adults and said it had identified a new generation of 'Potentialists' who rated the opportunity for fulfilment in life way beyond mere career ambition. It found that nine out of ten people believe it is important to follow their dreams 'alongside the demanding responsibilities of adult life' and that three quarters said they were looking for new ways to enrich their lives.

In a video during which she visited The School of

Life (which gives lectures on realising one's potential), Lorraine added: 'Some might say I have already reached my potential but I have not finished yet.' She said it wasn't just about job satisfaction or a change in career (of which none knew better than her!) but could be found in the simpler things such as 'spending more time with your kids, learning a foreign language or learning to play a musical instrument'. She concluded: 'It's really important to follow your dreams for personal reasons, fulfilment, satisfaction, and just to make life more fun. With some baby steps, trust me, it really is possible.'

Lorraine had been chosen to front the campaign because she is the 'ultimate Potentialist, constantly striving to realise her next aspiration or dream, as demonstrated through the fascinatingly diverse path that she has taken through her life and career.' She added: 'My inner voice can sometimes be quite negative, so it is about attempting to change that internal dialogue which sometimes says that you cannot do things. I suppose reading good books and being around positive people is a good way too; people that want to take you higher mentally and emotionally, as they are the building blocks to success in my opinion.'

On 25 February Lorraine was a guest speaker at The School of Life. The event was a sell-out. On a more personal level, she posted a message on Twitter saying that literature from the school had helped her 'make the leap' and that she recommended it to anyone who was 'stuck in a relationship/job rut and needed help to "get unstuck"'. She also posted a quotation, set as a verse, taken from an essay by Bessie A. Stanley, which seemed to have a poignant meaning for her:

To laugh often and love much;
To win the respect of intelligent persons
And the affection of children;
To earn the approbation of honest citizens
And endure the betrayal of false friends;
To appreciate beauty;
To find the best in others;
To leave the world a bit better,
Whether by a healthy child,
A garden patch or a redeemed social condition...
To know even one life has breathed easier,
Because you have lived –
This is to have succeeded.

Lorraine had certainly succeeded in another sale of her programme to foreign shores. New Zealand's Prime channel announced her first series *Baking Made Easy* would air in 2013. And as well as having her fourth cookery book as a work in progress, she was having meetings about 'some really exciting foodie and non-foodie projects.' The BBC stated how Lorraine was 'a very important talent for us' and hinted at 'projects in the pipeline' that would involve her. Meanwhile, another TV project – for the Sky Living channel – was announced at the end of February. The series, *My Kitchen Rules*, would each week see six amateur cook duos – husbands and wives, mothers and daughters or two best friends – at work in their own homes to see who could create the best dish. The challenges would get harder and end in a 'cook off' in the television studio.

Lorraine was to be one of the hosts and judges. Her fellow host was to be award-winning Michelin-starred chef Jason Atherton, famed for opening Gordon Ramsay's restaurant Maze and owner of Pollen Street Social restaurant in London's Mayfair. 'I am truly delighted to be working with renowned chef Jason Atherton. I am a huge fan of his beautiful food,' commented Lorraine, before adding: 'He is a very talented and exciting chef, which makes him the perfect co-host and judging partner for the show.' Atherton reciprocated the praise and said: 'I'm really looking forward to working with Lorraine... I can't wait to hit the road to meet some of the UK's most accomplished home cooks.'

Lorraine described the show as 'an exciting new venture' and said she was looking forward to 'stepping back from the oven... and judging other people's efforts'. She thanked Sky for the opportunity.

Interestingly, the Sky Living series was a version of the show already being seen in Australia – so perhaps Lorraine had had business talks about the venture on her last visit there.

Lorraine's optimistic start to the year was blighted by the death of her close friend Jeremy Paxton. The 53-year-old millionaire had suffered a fatal heart attack at his home in Caversham, Berkshire, on 5 February. Paxton was one of the many sponsors of Lorraine when she took part in the London run the year before, and had donated to the cause. Lorraine paid a tribute to him, describing him as an 'incredible friend' whose fund raising for good causes was an 'inspiration to many.'

Although Lorraine has often expressed her opinion on certain matters – such as the BNP's stance and of course, any issues concerning children in care – in March she entered the minefield of one controversial proposal that combined both politics and fostering issues. The British government's decision to impose a tax on spare bedrooms had already provoked the anger of many in receipt of housing benefit who said they could not afford the tax and would be forced to move to smaller homes. It also raised concerns with the Fostering Network, which said sibling groups in foster care could be unnecessarily split up as a result of the Government's 'failure to exempt their foster carers from housing benefit penalties'. The group said that foster children are not included when the number of occupants are counted in a property, and while welcoming exemption for one spare room, added that those in homes with two or more bedrooms for foster children faced housing benefit cuts.

Lorraine described the fears as 'a terrible thing' and asked how she could help. She also further confirmed her support to the fostering cause by once again helping to publicise the Fostering Network's Foster Care Fortnight in May 2013. She said: 'I want people to know that great foster carers helped me when I needed someone to be there for me the most. Growing up in and around the care system isn't easy.' She also urged people to put themselves 'in the frame' and consider being a foster carer.

In an interview with Lorraine Kelly on ITV's *Daybreak* on 13 May, Lorraine said: 'It's a great experience being in a situation where you need a home, and just have people come forward and welcome you in.' Of her first foster family, she described how there had been 'lots of love and caring and warmth and safety'. Her own experience made her realise how fostering can be both different and satisfying and she urged people to come forward to give a home to the 9,000 children who needed one. 'The kids get a lot out of it – it's challenging, rewarding and to be able to provide a loving home for a child is a wonderful thing to do,' she said. Lorraine announced she was also planning a documentary on fostering for the BBC and hinted there would be another cookery series, but not until the following year.

Another break out of the country saw Lorraine travelling to Sri Lanka in early April – in between the two days a week she was now working at her Cupcake Bakehouse – for a combined business trip and vacation that she described as a 'work, foodie fact-finding trip'. Her base was the Talalla Retreat boutique hotel in Gandarawatta, about four hours' drive from Columbo airport. Lorraine used the trip to research Sri Lankan dishes for her new book (she already had Sri Lankan chicken curry as one of her fans' favourites). She described her visit as 'a whistlestop tour', the only small mishap occurring when she mistook a stick for a snake and 'screamed the hotel down'. Thank goodness, said Lorraine afterwards, that she had chocolate coloured skin 'to hide my embarrassed red cheeks'.

At the end of the month, on 30 April, Lorraine attended the launch of the Care Inquiry, set up to improve the welfare of children in care. She was one of the speakers there, together with MP Ed Timpson. 'Wish me luck,' she tweeted. But she need not have worried for Emma Corbett, Participation Officer of The Who Cares? Trust congratulated Lorraine on her speech, saying she was 'fab', 'spoke from the heart' and did 'a great job championing the listening to each child as an individual'.

It was also in late April that Lorraine made a significant departure from the pressures of compiling her new book and filming for the new TV series. She put her care for children into action when she took a week off to undertake what she described as a 'humbling and inspiring' time with the Theraplay Institute, an American-based group that provides training 'for building and enhancing attachment, self-esteem, trust in others and joyful engagement' between adults and children. Its training is aimed at those who work in mental health, parents and teachers, and the institute states that it practises and teaches how to 'provide the best practice therapy for problems resulting from international adoption, trauma/abuse, development disorders, ADD/ADHD, reactive attachment disorder, medical trauma and others'. This was no courtesy visit, or indeed one taken out of curiosity. For Lorraine had a very serious intent – she embarked on the four-day training sessions, described as Level One and aimed at those who wish to learn the basics of the therapy. It was, she said, 'a highly effective mode of therapy for children and their carers'.

Lorraine did not say if she got involved in this for personal reasons or whether she is thinking of it as a serious prospect for the future. But it will be interesting to see if she decides to pursue the Theraplay training further – students can progress to higher levels to Theraplay Master Class – and drastically changes her life goals again.

Lorraine is today happy with her partner, former music company executive and divorced father of two, Ged Doherty, 55. But he was only allowed in her life when she felt her daughter Ella was ready to accept her having a new partner. There had been other men after her divorce, but none were important enough to warrant the big step of becoming part of her private world. Like other single mothers, Lorraine did not want to rush the often-fragile situation of a child meeting mum's man friend – 'It is quite exciting being a single mother. It can be an adventure. But you don't want to introduce your child to a new man until you are completely sure. It's a challenge.'

Lorraine and Doherty – who acted as chairman of The BRIT Awards from 2008 to 2010 and greatly boosted the televised programme's viewing figures – reportedly met through friends at dinner in London's Claridge's Hotel in 2009. Just like all relationships in Lorraine's life, this one has not been without its troubles. In July 2011 Doherty – described by a former colleague as 'one of the nicest men in the business' – lost his job as chairman and chief executive officer of the UK branch of Sony BMG. He had been with the company for 30 years and chairman since 2006, when a representative of rival Universal appeared on the scene and slashed the executive positions (Doherty was replaced by a former member of the group Dexys Midnight Runners). This was despite former student gig promoter Doherty once being hailed as having a 'happy knack' for increasing profits with the reputation of being a 'shrewd strategist', and working with some of the biggest names in the music business. He was also listed in the *Evening Standard*'s London's 1,000 most influential people in rock and pop in 2010. (In January of that year Sony had confirmed a 'long-term global venture' with music mogul Simon Cowell, leading Doherty to comment: 'I am absolutely delighted that we have been able to extend our long and mutually beneficial partnership with Simon. He is an inspiring and stimulating business partner and working with him closely over the last ten years has been an absolute pleasure.') Just seven months later Doherty would no longer be called on to comment on any matters concerning Sony...

Perhaps with Lorraine's encouragement Doherty learned that you may be down but you will never be out. At the end of 2011 he started his own production company, Break For It Media Limited. In February 2012 he also set up Raindog Films Limited of which he is director and management consultant.

But in a relationship it is the more personal involvement that really matters and Doherty was more than willing to prove to Lorraine that whatever was important to her was also important to him. In July 2012, he took part alongside her in the sponsored race the London run (completing it in 1hr 30mins and raising £7,750 through sponsorship which included such luminaries as Olympic champion marathon man Usain Bolt, who added the message 'I know you will do me proud') as well as sponsoring her for £125 with the message 'I'm proud of you') in support of Lorraine's charity TACT. (He also undertook a 150-mile 'golf/ride' to raise funds for the Multiple Sclerosis charity later that year.)

Although the couple spent a lot of time together it was a while before Lorraine trusted Doherty enough for him to spend less time at his flat and more at hers. She was always wary of relationships, fearing they would fail. Keeping her independence seemed at times to prevent her happiness ending, but the couple now mostly share her flat in Chelsea. Lorraine is trying, finally, to accept there are relationships that can last. She has said: 'I'm not someone who ever feels settled, although in the last few years I've felt more settled than ever before. I say "success is not final and failure is not fatal." I take every day as it comes and I don't like to look too far ahead. I don't know if it is going to last.' She naturally finds it hard to put total belief in anyone. 'It's not that I don't think I can form a secure bond – but it's always at the back of your mind.

You don't trust that anything will last. What I've done is accepted that it's part of who I am. I don't try to fight it any more.'

Something that enforces Lorraine's newly acquired trust in anyone close to her – as well as the ring she sports on her engagement finger – is that Doherty also became general secretary of Mint and Lime Limited, the company registered in Lorraine's former married name and of which she has been a director since its formation in May 2010. Described as handling television programme production activities, the company took Doherty on board in September 2011. He replaced Andrew Antonio, who had been general secretary since the start of the company (appointed company secretary of Cupcake Bakehouse in February 2010, Antonio still remains in that position). Although the company address given for Lorraine is in Burnham-on-Sea in Somerset, Doherty's is given as Beaufort Street, Chelsea, London.

Mint and Lime, like most companies, has varied fortunes and although there is a healthy bank balance of nearly £1.5m, liabilities and money owing give it a value of a not-too-staggering figure of £129,617. It may be some time before Lorraine fulfils her wish for more Bakehouses. Accounts filed in October 2012 show that the company owed over £56,000 to creditors (and was owed more than £14,000 by trade debtors) and that its 'book value' – what the company is worth – was minus £45,486.

Lorraine has said that her best times are at home with her family 'cooking lovely meals and having lots of friends around.' She also feels that in a financial climate where money is not so readily available to spend on the pleasures of life such as eating out, people 'have realised how lovely it is to have a group of friends round and present them with something they've made themselves. It's cheaper than going to a restaurant.' And of course, there is the opportunity for Lorraine to impress with her cake making – 'Everyone says "Wow" when you bring a cake to the table. It's a good time for cake!'

These invitations are rarely returned, not because friends don't wish to take their turn in hosting Lorraine, but because they are nervous about matching up to her in the kitchen. Instead, if they want to have dinner with her then they invite her out to a restaurant. Lorraine has said that their fears are totally unfounded and she would love to be cooked for, promising to be 'kind, supportive, helpful and encouraging', so maybe they should be braver – although there is always Lorraine's natural urge to try to take over when others are cooking, something she has said she needs to control! But in the enviable position of being able to do so, eating out is one of life's pleasures for Lorraine anyway, and she has admitted going to Michelin-starred restaurants two or three times a month.

If there are spare days in her frenzied schedule,

Lorraine will go back to her old home town to watch Witney Football Club play or escape to luxury hotels such as Babington House in Somerset or The Grove in Hertfordshire. Both provide an excellent opportunity to unwind – and form part of a lifestyle Lorraine could only have dreamt about in the past. (There was once a time when she and daughter Ella went to the Maldives for a holiday which was so expensive that Lorraine joked they would have to live on potatoes for the rest of the year.) Lorraine can now afford to eat regularly at her favourite restaurant Le Gavroche in London, which she first discovered back in 1999 and has described as 'old-school, decadent and luxurious', 'the best restaurant on earth'. Owner Michel Roux Jnr (her favourite chef) made her a belated special 40th birthday dessert.

Lorraine celebrated this landmark birthday on 17 November 2012. As well as an evening party for friends (she took pains to draw up a suitable playlist of her favourite music), she also enjoyed a champagne afternoon tea at Fortnum & Mason hosted by Fortnum's chief executive Ewan Ventners (the man behind getting her cakes into Selfridges), who had joined the store in July that year and with whom Lorraine had stayed in contact. Completing her birthday celebrations was the announcement that Lorraine had been signed up by the *Sun* as their weekly Sunday columnist. 'Lorraine has now joined the *Sun* family, offering readers recipes and cooking tips every Sunday. She says: "It's a great privilege to be a columnist for the best-selling paper in the country. *Sun* readers love their food and are the smartest critics around. They know what they like and what works for them and their families. If I can help them with some ideas – including ones that will really work on a budget – I'd be delighted. I can't wait to get stuck in." And Lorraine would love to hear YOUR favourite foodie ideas. She adds: "I want to hear from *Sun* readers. Something tells me they will have some brilliant ideas to share and I want to know how they get on with my recipes."'

And of course Lorraine's own Cupcake Bakehouse did not forget the big birthday. Staff made a beautiful cake with brilliant white icing topped with red candles, perched on two tiers of colourful cupcakes, and with more cupcakes around the base. The caption 'We made some extra special birthday cakes for Lorraine Pascale's birthday yesterday. Here's how our boss likes it!' accompanied the picture of their creation on Facebook (along with birthday greetings from some of Lorraine's fans).

Despite her origins and the problems she has had to face Lorraine is happy in her own skin. She still cannot work out why male fans are so effusive about her looks – and why some women are so envious – but she works hard to look good for her own self-esteem and because she knows not looking her best on television and at public appearances would have the critics come out in force. (People comment on how tired she looks if she doesn't cover up the natural dark pigmentation under her eyes with concealer.) And the secret of looking so stunning, and her glowing skin? 'I think it is the truck loads of makeup I put on it!' She has said she is happy to get older and is as yet wrinkle-free (perhaps this is down to the Q10 anti-wrinkle cream she uses at night). For beauty followers, Lorraine also uses Avène skincare products, Bliss facial scrub and L'Occitane shea butter – which she describes as her 'best winter product' for her hair, face and body. One of her newest beauty discoveries is the 'Black Up' range – 'Needless to say the make-up is for the woman "of colour" as they say Stateside.' She also takes a range of vitamins.

Despite always looking straight, sleek and shining, Lorraine's natural Afro hair, which she describes as 'like a microphone' – is still her biggest beauty bugbear. It measures a metre across and has a habit of shaping into an oblong if she leans on something! Said Lorraine: 'You're constantly trying to pat it into a circle otherwise it's a strange four-sided shape. It's untameable.' It's not a look she would wish to be seen with and so she regularly has it straightened and wears extensions 'which look after themselves'.

She ensures her teenage daughter Ella enjoys the

happiness and security that she herself never had and the two are exceptionally close. Despite her hectic life Lorraine still makes Ella her priority (fitting in time to prepare her for her mock GCSE exams, and the 'real' ones which Ella did well in). And they share a love of travelling – although things don't always go according to plan. Once, when they flew off for a last-minute Christmas break to the Dominican Republic in 2011, the outward journey was anything but relaxing. Ella has inherited her mother's lanky height and the two were forced to stand for most of the flight because the seats were so tightly packed! The plane was then diverted, meaning nearly a whole day's travel. When they finally reached what they had hoped would be a top-notch hotel their expectations were cruelly dashed. It was, Lorraine had to confess, 'horrible' and the meals sorely tested the sensitivities of a conscientious chef. 'The food was horrendous. It was served in a buffet which can be fine but there were kids running up, shoving their hands in and tossing half-eaten sausages back in…' Ella must have been equally horrified for she initially shared her mother's passion for cooking (other teenage pastimes eventually took over!) and the two spent time together 'bonding' in the kitchen.

Lorraine finds comfort in looking at her daughter and seeing her own flesh and blood. 'There's something about seeing my own features in her that's reassuring,' she has said. Ella has her mother's slim build and height (give or take an extra centimetre or two) and has even inherited the trademark gap-toothed smile. Lorraine has confessed that she had her gap filled in a little (when she started modelling she could fit a pound coin and a ten pence piece in the gap) but she refuses to give in to her daughter's requests to do the same – 'She says we should have a deal that she will get her teeth done if I have Botox, but I tell her no way.'

Ella's build has also helped her do well at sport. She is a good runner and javelin thrower. The love and pride Lorraine has for Ella shines through. She says with a mother's natural warmth that although her daughter looks like her, Ella is more beautiful. A large photograph of mother and daughter has pride of place on the mantelpiece in Lorraine's flat. But Lorraine is insistent that she does not embark on a career as a model – 'I think that there are so many things one can do these days especially for her as she is so intelligent!' Although Ella nowadays has lost some of the interest in cooking she once shared with Lorraine, whatever career choice she finally makes will always have her mother's support.

After her traumatic early life, Lorraine has said that she feels positive about the future. With culinary success, TV stardom and a happy family life, she certainly does seem to have found happiness at last.